THE LIFE HISTORY OF THE UNITED STATES

Volume 5: 1849-1865

THE UNION SUNDERED

TIME
LIFE
BOOKS ®

THE ART OF SEWING

THE OLD WEST

THE EMERGENCE OF MAN

THE AMERICAN WILDERNESS

THE TIME-LIFE ENCYCLOPEDIA OF GARDENING

LIFE LIBRARY OF PHOTOGRAPHY

THIS FABULOUS CENTURY

FOODS OF THE WORLD

TIME-LIFE LIBRARY OF AMERICA

TIME-LIFE LIBRARY OF ART

GREAT AGES OF MAN

LIFE SCIENCE LIBRARY

THE LIFE HISTORY OF THE UNITED STATES

TIME READING PROGRAM

LIFE NATURE LIBRARY

LIFE WORLD LIBRARY

FAMILY LIBRARY:

 THE TIME-LIFE BOOK OF THE FAMILY CAR

 THE TIME-LIFE FAMILY LEGAL GUIDE

 THE TIME-LIFE BOOK OF FAMILY FINANCE

THE LIFE HISTORY OF THE UNITED STATES

Consulting Editor, Henry F. Graff

Volume 5: 1849-1865

THE UNION SUNDERED

by T. Harry Williams

and the Editors of

TIME-LIFE BOOKS

TIME-LIFE BOOKS, NEW YORK

THE AUTHOR, T. Harry Williams, has devoted his professional career—as teacher, writer and editor—to the history of the Civil War, on which he is a leading expert. Born in Vinegar Hill, Illinois, he has been living in the South since 1941. He earned his Ph.D. at the University of Wisconsin; since 1953 he has been Boyd Professor of History at Louisiana State University. His book *Huey Long* received the 1969 National Book Award and the Pulitzer Prize for biography. He is also the author of *Lincoln and His Generals*, a definitive work on command problems; *Lincoln and the Radicals;* and *P.G.T. Beauregard.* He has edited two collections of Abraham Lincoln papers.

THE CONSULTING EDITOR for this series, Henry F. Graff, is Professor of History at Columbia University in New York.

Valuable assistance in preparing this volume was given by Roger Butterfield, who served as picture consultant; Editorial Production, Norman Airey; Library, Benjamin Lightman; Picture Collection, Doris O'Neil; Photographic Laboratory, George Karas; TIME-LIFE News Service, Murray J. Gart. Revisions Staff: Harold C. Field, Joan Chambers.

CONTENTS

A NOTE TO THE READER: The story of the Civil War is related in two volumes of this series. This volume reports the political events of the period. Volume 6 contains accounts of the war's military events. —THE EDITORS

1. THE FATEFUL DIVISION

THE America of the 1850s was a thriving, booming country—but under the surface there simmered a regional conflict that in another decade would erupt into violent warfare. The attitudes of North and South were being set in rigid and hostile molds: by mid-century Northerners and Southerners viewed each other as different, inferior and dangerous. A visitor from another planet might have received the impression that sometimes comes to the modern researcher in the angry documents: that the antislavery North and the slaveholding South were more like two nations engaged in a cold war than parts of the same nation.

From both sections there issued bold assertions of cultural superiority. "The Southern character," said one Northern critic, "is infinitely boastful, vainglorious, full of dash, without endurance, treacherous, cunning, timid, and revengeful." "The Southern plantations," said another, "are little less than Negro harems." And a third: "Their civilization is a mermaid—lovely and languid above, but ending in bestial deformity."

Southern analyses of the North were conducted at the same level. "Free Society!" exclaimed a Georgia editor. "We sicken at the name. What is it but a conglomeration of greasy mechanics, filthy operatives, small-fisted farmers, and moon-struck theorists?" Northern society was common and faceless, cried one orator, but the men of the South were of a master race. "If there be a hope for the North—a hope that she will ever ride the waves of bottomless

SOLDIER PRESIDENT Zachary Taylor wears the uniform he distinguished during the Mexican War. He died in office at a portentous moment, amid the 1850 debate on slavery.

perdition that roll around her—it is the fact that the South will stand by her and will lend a hand to rescue her."

The simple fact is that the United States of the 1850s was not a nation in the sense in which the word would later be used. It was what its name indicated, an association of states with common interests. The extent to which they were united under a central government was defined differently in the North and the South. Generally the North favored more centralism, the South less. But both assumed that any change would develop within the framework of the existing association. Not even the most ardent Northern advocates of a stronger government would use the word "nation" to characterize their ideal. With a significance they did not realize, they spoke instead, and would so speak until near the end of the Civil War, of "the Union."

Y ET the states were in many meaningful ways united. Their people shared a common historical experience. Americans of all sections were proud of the national past—of the Declaration of Independence and the Revolution and its godlike heroes; of the equally godlike Fathers and their Constitution; of the second war with Britain for neutral rights and the war with Mexico for empire; and of the irresistible sweep of American dominion over the continent to the Pacific coast. It was a young country, still astonishingly close to its origins. Of the two great military leaders of the Civil War, Robert E. Lee could recall his boyhood associations with his father, Colonel "Light-Horse Harry" Lee, one of the shining figures of the Revolutionary army, and Ulysses S. Grant had a grandfather who had been a captain in the Revolution.

Besides a shared pride in their past, the American people also had a territorial identity: their land was a definite and obvious physical entity. They spoke the same language and had much the same cultural heritage and outlook. Although they were of diverse religions, most belonged to variants of the Christian faith, and although religious prejudice abounded it was not a divisive influence. The American people were of essentially similar ethnic composition. Of the total population of 23 million in 1850, about two and a quarter million were of alien birth, having arrived during the first great wave of European immigration, from 1830 on. In the next wave of the '50s another 2.8 million would come over, most of them, like their predecessors from the first wave, from Ireland and Germany. Their presence aroused some nativist resentment among descendants of the older English stock, but the newcomers were similar enough to those already here so that, after some initial difficulty, they succeeded in merging into the common mass.

In all sections Americans subscribed to a set of principles so completely accepted as to constitute almost a national creed. They believed that man was a special being with a higher nature and was therefore capable of great, perhaps limitless progress; that a supernatural power, God or some impersonal force, ordered the affairs of men to a predestined and happy end; that this supreme power had revealed to men a higher law and that their own Constitution was the closest human approximation to the divine statute; that the ownership of private property was the soundest basis for a prosperous economic system; that thrift and acquisitiveness were among the noblest of the virtues; and that the American experiment in popular government was infinitely precious, unique among the nations, and the hope of all mankind for a brighter future.

The concept that America had a world mission was the most moving article

Immigrants land at the Battery in 1847 in a painting by Samuel B. Waugh. The refugees were welcomed by some, eyed suspiciously by others. Though the Order of the Star-Spangled Banner (precursor of the Know-Nothing party) wanted "America for the Americans," Walt Whitman happily saw the U.S. as "not merely a nation, but a teeming nation of nations."

in the national faith. None caught its meaning better than a politician from the Western prairies. Abraham Lincoln spoke of America's destiny in words that reverberate down through the years. The United States was an idea, Lincoln said, and that idea was the sentiment of equality in the Declaration of Independence that gave "liberty, not alone to the people of this country, but hope to the world for all future time. It was that which gave promise that in due time the weights should be lifted from the shoulders of all men, and that *all* should have an equal chance." The American Union was "the last, best hope of earth," he said.

Such were the bonds that bound the United States, and they were close and compelling, not to be lightly or easily broken. If the American states did not comprise a nation, they were at least a cohesive political, economic and social community. If the national government was not a mighty or pervasive power that affected the daily lives of its people—nine tenths of them had not paid a tax of any kind, tariffs excepted, for over 30 years—it was always present in men's minds as a symbol of American greatness. If the American people did not give an undivided and unswerving loyalty to the government in Washington, they were yet proudly conscious of their national character.

An overweening pride in all things American was, in fact, a marked quality of all Americans. They bragged about everything, most loudly about the size of their country, its towering mountains, its mighty rivers and its boundless limits. In their assurance they could laugh at their own excesses. At an international gathering, one story ran, a Bostonian rose and offered a toast: "Here's to the United States, bounded on the north by British America, on the south by Mexico, on the east by the Atlantic Ocean, and on the west by the Pacific Ocean." Next came a Chicagoan who proposed: "My friend has too limited a view. We must look to our Manifest Destiny. Here's to the United States, bounded on the north by the North Pole, on the south by the South Pole, on the east by the rising and on the west by the setting sun." Then a Californian got up and asked: "With Manifest Destiny in our favor, why limit ourselves so narrowly? I give you the United States, bounded on the north by the Aurora Borealis, on the south by the Precession of the Equinoxes, on the east by Primeval Chaos—and on the west by the Day of Judgment."

The American debut of the beautiful European dancer Lola Montez in 1851 briefly diverted and scandalized the country. Few attended her performances, as is apparent in this lithograph, but her amorous links to such figures as Franz Liszt and Czar Nicholas I made New Yorkers flock to her private "receptions" to shake her hand and talk with her—at one dollar per head.

And it is true that Americans had much to boast about in the 1850s. The years of that decade witnessed an unparalleled expansion of America's material resources. Between 1850 and 1860 the population increased by more than eight million to a total of 31.5 million. The value of manufactured goods rose from slightly over a billion dollars to $1,885,000,000, and the value of farm products from $900 million to $1,910,000,000. The number of manufacturing establishments jumped from 123,000 to more than 140,000, and the number of farms from one and a half million to two million. Most sensational of all, the total railroad mileage more than tripled—from 9,000 to 30,000.

This burst of productive energy was not confined to the material realm. The American creative spirit flourished in other areas, in science and journalism and oratory, and most notably in literature. The great authors of the past two decades added to their fame, and new writers emerged to fashion new reputations. From the New England school, still lustily creative, came a stream of works. Ralph Waldo Emerson, Henry Wadsworth Longfellow, Nathaniel Hawthorne, Oliver Wendell Holmes—all were close to the peak of their powers, and most were optimistic about man's future in America. If some of the newer literary figures—Herman Melville, Henry David Thoreau, Walt Whitman—were more sharply aware of the numerous imperfections in American society, they nevertheless had faith that their vigorous land could eventually create a happier community for the whole human family. "Liberty, let others despair of you," cried Whitman, "—I never despair of you."

Most Northern writers after 1850 trained some of their sharpest barbs at slavery and the South, and Southern authors responded in kind. One, William J. Grayson, composed 1,600 lines in heroic couplets to demonstrate that the slave enjoyed a better life than the Northern laborer. ("The cabin home, not comfortless, though rude, / Light daily labor, and abundant food, / The sturdy health that temperate habits yield, / the cheerful song that rings in every field. . . .") Still, down to the latest years of the decade American literature was primarily national and nonpolitical in theme and outlook.

One of the first great industrialists, Peter Cooper began as a glue manufacturer, acting as his own stoker, bookkeeper and salesman. After virtually monopolizing the glue market, he turned to producing iron in a crude foundry like that shown below. With the fortune he amassed in these and his later ventures, he became one of America's leading philanthropists.

THESE prosperous and productive United States, expanding on all fronts and stretching their boundaries to the Pacific coast, were being drawn into an ever closer communion by the forces of science. The inventions and discoveries and devices of previous years—the steamboat, the cotton gin, the canals, the railroads, the beginnings of mass production in industry—were forcing union whether men wanted it or not. It was the modern world taking shape, and there was an awesome inevitability about it.

This technological revolution culminated in the '50s with the emergence of a truly national system of transportation and communication. The central element in the system was the growing network of railroads. Spanning the Eastern half of the country, 30,000 miles of track reached out from the Atlantic Coast cities to the upper Mississippi Valley. At a few points the iron rails were even pushing west of the great river. Of the total trackage, 20,000 miles were concentrated in the Northeast and the Northwest, and the largest and longest lines, the "trunks," ran between these sections. The effect of this pattern of distribution was to lessen dependence on the Mississippi River as an artery of commerce, to channel intersectional trade in an east-west direction, and to bind the North together into a conscious economic province. In all sections, the coming of the railroads had an almost magical impact on time and space. In the early years of the century a trip from New York to St. Louis by stage and riverboat consumed over three weeks. By 1850 it could be made by rail and water in twelve and a half days, by 1857 by rail alone in two.

The transportation revolution was an economic phenomenon, but its import was not lost on the politicians. Senator Stephen A. Douglas of Illinois, who understood material expansion much better than he did the morality of the slavery issue, saw in the railroads a promise of greater national unity. Because of them, Douglas pointed out, the remotest parts of the country were closer to the center than when there were only 13 states.

Douglas' estimate did not quite hold for the farthest American possessions. Beyond the line of frontier expansion, the tier of states just west of the Mississippi, few permanent settlements existed until California and Oregon were reached. But over this trackless expanse of mountains, deserts and plains, remarkably rapid transport was maintained with the Pacific provinces.

The jolting stagecoaches of the Overland Mail Company, bearing both passengers and mail, made regular runs between St. Louis and San Francisco in

25 days. Even faster was the Pony Express, established in 1860 by the great freighting company of Russell, Majors and Waddell, which carried only mail. Whereas a stagecoach could average 100 to 125 miles every 24 hours, the pony rider covered 250 miles. Relays of riders flew all the way from St. Joseph, Missouri, to Sacramento in 10 days. Mark Twain, traveling west by coach, saw a rider of the Express dash by the doors and then vanish in the distance, and he never forgot the sight. "So sudden is it all, and so like a flash of unreal fancy, that but for the flake of white foam left quivering and perishing on a mail sack after the vision had flashed by and disappeared, we might have doubted whether we had seen any actual horse and man at all, maybe." But the Pony Express never turned a profit; the experiment lasted only 18 months.

Theoretically it was possible by the late 1850s for a traveler to cross the continent in 27 days—two by train from New York to St. Louis and 25 more by coach to the coast—although in practice nobody could have survived such a continuous trek. The average traveler, the migrant seeking a new home and carrying his household goods with him in a wagon, required 150 days to move from ocean to ocean. (As a mark of the sustained influence of technology, when the railroads to the coast were completed in 1869, the average time would be cut to six days.)

There was also a revolution in communications. Just as the railroads answered the needs of a large country for long-distance transportation, so the telegraph solved the problem of extended communication. By 1861 over 50,000 miles of wire linked all sections of the country, including the two coasts. The telegraph had an immediate influence on the dissemination of news and thereby helped strengthen the ties of nationalism.

At that time there was no magazine or newspaper that could be said to be a national organ—that is, read by large numbers of people in all sections. But there were more than 3,000 newspapers, and they reached tremendous regional audiences. More than any other medium the papers molded public opinion, and in the '50s those in the larger cities began to take on a common emphasis and a common form. They still carried an abundance of political news, as in previous decades, but they gave increasing attention to what later would be called human interest items, to what one enterprising editor cheerfully described as "a most interesting record of horrid murders, outrageous robberies, bold forgeries, astounding burglaries, hideous rapes, vulgar seductions." Now, because of the telegraph, the press could report events almost instantaneously. The first great American news service, the Associated Press, was founded in 1848. The American people, wherever they lived, read the same news at the same time, and this too was a unifying factor in their society.

Charles Goodyear, who made rubber popular and durable, existed from hand to mouth for years while perfecting his process; Mrs. Goodyear had to make her bonnets of pasteboard. Even after he patented his "vulcanized" rubber, and showed it at London's 1851 Crystal Palace exhibition (below), creditors pursued him. Goodyear died, still deep in debt, in 1860.

THEY were the United States, and they were also the different and the divided states. In their social structures all showed many variations from one another. But the differences between individual states were minor and of no great political import. The divergence that was serious was between groups of states, each acting as an entity and calling itself a section.

There were three of these sections in 1850—the Northeast, comprising New England and the Middle Atlantic states; the Northwest, extending around the Great Lakes from Ohio to Minnesota; and the South, including all the slave states and stretching from Maryland to Texas. Each section exhibited certain common features of climate, soil and terrain, and each had recognizable and in a sense logical boundaries. But no one of them, it has to be emphasized, was a natural physical province. To be sure, nature had something to do with creating the sections, but they were also the result of history, accident, economics and men. All these elements had joined their influence to determine that each section would develop in a particular way—like the others and yet significantly different. These distinctive factors had invested each section with a peculiar quality of its own—in each region one economic activity dominated material life, one set of moral values decided social standards and one class enjoyed more prestige and power than others.

It was this quality of oneness, this concentration of particular attitudes within geographic areas, that was the most distinctive and ominous feature of sectionalism. No one of the sections was completely monolithic, although the South eventually approached absolute unity. Each one had its inner differences and divisions. But each had also a remarkable cohesion and a capacity to close ranks for fundamental objectives. This was most evident in the sectional attitudes on economic issues. Each section tended to take a unitary position on economic questions, to push its own pet legislation in Congress. And because of sectionalism, ordinary variances became something dangerous and abnormal. When, for instance, the Northeast and the South clashed over the tariff, it was not just two rival economic powers contending for advantage—it was the people of two sections looking at each other suspiciously and angrily over a geographic line.

Economic sectionalism made every economic difference harder to adjust and complicated every dispute between the sections. It became a part of the struggle for political ascendancy. "You desire to weaken the political power of the southern states," Senator Jefferson Davis of Mississippi cried accusingly at the Northeast, "and why? Because you want, by an unjust system of legislation, to promote the industry of the New England states, at the expense of the people of the South and their industry." When economics was combined with the moral issue of slavery, the cycle was complete. For Joshua R. Giddings, a relentlessly antislavery congressman from Ohio, the connection was simple. The tariff, proclaimed Giddings, was an antislavery measure because it opposed the interest of those who upheld an evil institution. Then he asked what for him was the clinching question. "Are the farmers of the West . . . to give up the sale of their beef, pork, and flour, in order to increase the profits of those who raise children for sale, and deal in the bodies of women?"

THE Northeast was a land of factories and spindles and lathes, of manufacturers and merchants and bankers. It was the industrial section, and the men of business comprised its reigning class. Other occupations and classes in its social structure consisted mainly of a growing mass of laborers, most of them unskilled and unorganized in trade unions, and a proportionately declining farm population, unable to compete with the more fertile Northwest. Here too, centered in Massachusetts and New York, were the most vigorous and vocal intellectual and literary circles in the country, their members fiercely denunciatory of slavery, yet not sure on the other hand that they liked the ideals of the business civilization growing up around them.

But regardless of the doubts of authors or of the aristocrats in old established families, industry was on the march in the Northeast, and the leaders of industry were beginning to join the merchant princes and the bankers in

Walt Whitman chose this picture of himself as the frontispiece for "Leaves of Grass," published in 1855. While writing the book Whitman worked with his father as a housebuilder. He appeared everywhere in the denims of the carpenter, wearing a Quaker hat, with his shirt left open at the throat. Though 1,000 copies of his book were printed, only a few dozen sold.

occupying the seats of economic power. Of the 140,000 factories in the country, 74,000 were in this section, and they were larger in every way than those in other areas. They represented well over half the nation's total capital investment in all industry, and the annual value of their products was two thirds of the national total. They exported practically nothing abroad, disposing of their goods in the American market and especially in the Northwest.

The industrial capitalists constituted a sort of hierarchy in the Northeast; more and more they were reaching for political power. They sometimes disagreed among themselves; they were not without critics and opponents, and in some contests for power they had to compromise or even yield. Still they consistently maintained their influence, partly because they did not hesitate to use their wealth in politics and partly because they were respected merely because they had wealth. They led too by consent, because they and the masses had no fundamental differences. On most national issues, opinion in the Northeast tended to agree regardless of the individual's social or economic status.

As an industrial region, the Northeast favored a policy of government aid to business—a protective tariff, internal improvements (transportation projects financed by the national government), adequate but controlled bank credit—and generally its congressional representatives of both parties pressed for these objectives. The political leaders of the Northeast, the men who represented business, were much more interested in economics than in political theory. Nobody voiced their views more accurately than Daniel Webster, who for years embodied the section's philosophy in the United States Senate. Basically conservative, Webster yet had no fears of a democratic majority threatening property. A strong government acting constantly to expand the economy would, he believed, have the effect of so diffusing wealth throughout the system that no dangerous class divisions would appear. Webster liked to talk about giving an economic interest to the laborer. "He thereby obtains a feeling of respectability, a sense of propriety and of personal independence which is generally essential to elevated character. He has a stake in society, and is inclined, therefore, rather to uphold than to demolish it."

The great majority of people of all classes in the Northeast were in some degree antislavery. If only a fraction were outright abolitionists, nearly all condemned the institution in theory. Some businessmen, to be sure, especially those with Southern trade interests, deprecated agitation of the slavery question. Said one prominent New York merchant to an abolitionist: "We cannot afford, sir, to let you and your associates succeed in your endeavor to overthrow slavery. It is not a matter of principle with us. It is a matter of business necessity." But as the '50s wore on and the economic split between North and South grew wider, "business necessity" ceased to bulk so large, and morality—often combined with such material issues as the tariff—came to outweigh all other considerations affecting the slavery issue.

When editor Horace Greeley (right) said "Go West, young man," his friend Joshua Bushnell Grinnell (left) followed the advice literally. He went to Iowa—though Greeley had meant Erie, Pennsylvania— and in 1854 founded the town there that bears his name. Greeley did not originate the expression "Go West"; he merely quoted it from an article in a Terre Haute newspaper.

THE Northwest, in contrast to the Northeast, was a section of farms and farmers, of grain and stock animals, of throbbing expansion and of even more expansive dreams for the future. It was an agricultural section; it had its growing metropolitan centers—Chicago, St. Louis, Cincinnati—but its population was primarily rural. It had also a developing factory system—a total of 37,000 plants employing over 200,000 workers—but its industry was small compared with the East's and its manufactured products largely related to agriculture: farm machines, packed meat, flour and leather. Among some Americans, Cincinnati was referred to as "Porkopolis," and an appalled visitor from Albany noted that at a reception given by a distinguished Chicagoan he met "out of a company of 36 men, 10 pork packers, three butchers, four railroad men," as well as "two bankers, one lawyer, eight doctors and a number of clerks." (He also commented unbelievingly that a "prominent fiddler" showed up at the same affair, "dressed in swallowtails, a checked vest, green necktie and red gloves.")

On its small, family-sized farms, averaging 160 acres, the West produced corn, wheat, cattle, sheep and hogs. The concentration of these items was a response to economic and sectional requirements. As the Northeast moved into its industrial and urban stage, it became increasingly an importer of food, and the logical source from which to import was the Northwest, close at hand and connected with the manufacturing section by the railroad network. It was also logical that the Northwest should obtain its finished goods from the Northeast, and so between the two sections a mutually profitable trade flowed in an always swelling stream. The economic relationship inevitably drew the Northern sections together in closer political alliance, and by creating a self-sustaining domestic market it strengthened the bases of nationalism.

No prestigious minority dominated Northwestern society the way the business community did the Northeast. The Northwest was, in the broadest sense, a democratic section. Practically all adult white men possessed the vote and most farmers owned their own land. Class lines were the most fluid in the country, and political life and preferment were open to all.

But although Western leaders talked a great deal about equality and the small man, and indulged in free and frequent denunciation of the rich and the powerful, their equalitarianism was not nearly so radical as it might seem. The democracy of the West was in reality a small capitalist philosophy and as such was basically conservative. It was highly property-conscious and placed a premium on the virtues of thrift and acquisitiveness. When Westerners talked about equality, they meant equality of economic opportunity, the right of all to acquire property in a fair competition. Their notion of an ideal society was one in which all those with ability and energy had secured property and those with special talents were getting more. Abraham Lincoln, who liked to recall that he began life as a hired laborer, expressed perfectly the economic philosophy of his section: "There is no permanent class of hired laborers amongst us. . . . The hired laborer of yesterday labors on his own account today; and will hire others to labor for him to-morrow. Advancement—improvement in condition—is the order of things in a society of equals."

THE Northwest might have its inner divisions, its political quarrels—the southern counties of Illinois, Indiana and Ohio had been settled by people from the South and the northern counties by people from the Northeast, and sometimes these sectional origins affected views on current issues—but like the Northeast it had a remarkable unity and a capacity to pursue common objectives. In national politics it strove for internal improvements, cheap or free public lands, and easy and abundant bank credit. It had no strong views on the tariff, although there were protectionist centers throughout the section, and over the years it had traded votes on this issue in return for support

At mid-century, Chicago buildings were considered "solid, lofty and in the most recent taste." This 1866 lithograph shows one such structure at Clark and Water Streets. Yet, for all the decorous architecture, Chicago's streets were so muddy that portions of its sidewalks had to be raised to clear the puddles. The city became notorious for its awkward sidewalk steps.

of its own measures. Sometimes the trading was with the Northeast (a high tariff for internal improvements), sometimes with the South (a low tariff for internal improvements).

But as time went on it became easier and more logical for the two Northern sections to join forces, both on the tariff question and in a general working alliance. They had a basis for cooperation in their trade relationship, and they had obvious common economic objectives—a tariff and internal improvements would benefit both. They were, although in different degree and for somewhat different reasons, antislavery. People in the Northwest had much the same outlook on slavery as those in the Northeast—they thought it was wrong and hoped it would ultimately be ended. The Western attitude was, however, less urgent and less moral and had in it less concern for the Negro; it was reflected in state laws that imposed harsher restrictions on black citizens than was the practice in the East. The West opposed the expansion of slavery, but in large part its position expressed no more than a reluctance to encounter the competition of black labor in the territories. Still, on the slavery question both Northern sections looked to the possibility of change. They looked to change in most areas of social action as well. The Northeast and the Northwest were modern, progressive. Their way would be the way of the future. In this they stood in significant contrast to their neighbor to the south.

THE South was a region of plantations and farms, of cotton and tobacco and sugar. In its southernmost regions it was a land of heat and rain and lush, almost tropical, foliage. It was pre-eminently the agricultural section, more pervasively rural and agrarian than even the Northwest. It was the only section in America that housed in large numbers a race of another color and that lived with a race problem, and by 1860 it was one of the few areas in all Western civilization that sustained the institution of human slavery (the only others were Brazil, Dutch Guiana and the Spanish colonies of Cuba and Puerto Rico). Of the three major American sections, the South was the one that deviated most sharply from the national pattern, and its differences were so obvious as to arrest attention in all sections. To Northerners the South did not seem progressive and flexible but backward and conservative and stubbornly opposed to needed change; it did not conform and it seemed to defy congruity. Most Southerners were aware that their society was distinctive, and they affected to believe that the difference made for superiority —the South, in contrast to the bustling and revolutionary North, was stable, orderly and sound.

Only a few particularly introspective individuals realized that their section was fast becoming an anomaly. "God forgive us," Mrs. Mary Boykin Chesnut of Camden, South Carolina, confided to her diary, "but ours is a monstrous system, a wrong and an iniquity!" Not many Southerners could have brought themselves to say openly what one Virginian said of his state's social system: "It has no parallel except in the other slaveholding states . . . and when closely inspected, looks very much like the remnant of an old civilization—a fragment of the feudal system floating about here on the bosom of the 19th Century."

Most Southerners had an entirely different picture of their society—it was perfect; it held a hope for the rest of the world; it pointed the way to the future. No man presented the picture of the flawless South with as much conviction as the lean ascetic from South Carolina who was the spokesman

Slaughterhouse workers spear cattle in an early Chicago scene. At first animals were kept in local tavern yards, but by 1865 the great stockyards were opened and Chicago had become "Butcher for the world." The 1865 yards housed 100,000 livestock, while the cattlemen who had brought them stayed at the Transit, a hotel offering two steaks and trimmings for 50 cents.

of the Southern mind. Senator John C. Calhoun believed with an icy intellectual passion that slavery, by preventing conflicts between capital and labor, provided the basis for the most stable social order that existed anywhere. "Hence the harmony, the union and stability of that section," Calhoun exclaimed. "The blessing of this state of things extends beyond the limits of the South. It makes that section the balance of the system; the great conservative power, which prevents other portions, less fortunately constituted, from rushing into conflict." As the '50s opened, not all Southerners accepted the conclusion of Calhoun's thought—that the South should never change, that it had no need to make any compromise with the modern world. But their acceptance would not be long in coming.

IN Northern eyes the section below the Potomac and the Ohio appeared to be a region of singular uniformity, an unbroken surface of concord and concert, and this was the way the South liked to think of itself. There was exaggeration in both the outside and the inside view. Within its vast expanse —in size it was the largest of the sections—the South presented an immense variety in every aspect of its being, in some respects more variety than the other two sections.

Although it had a certain physiographic uniformity—primarily a warm climate and a long growing season—the South exhibited, from one part to another, extremes of temperature and contrasts of terrain. Although its people in preponderant majority were Anglo-Saxon and Protestant and attached to the soil, they differed in significant ways—in their economic status and particular forms of agricultural occupation, in their political beliefs and loyalties, and in their social concepts and values.

Nor was this agricultural region exclusively devoted to agrarian ideals. It too could show its factories and its business class. The '50s witnessed an exuberant flowering of Southern industrial facilities. At the end of the decade 20,000 plants dotted the region, and the annual value of manufactured products reached $155,500,000, an increase over 10 years of nearly 97 per cent. Southern factories were selective in their products, concentrating on cotton textiles, flour and tobacco, and most of them were small in comparison with those of the Northeast. This was just the beginning of an industrial order, but it was a promising beginning that possibly heralded a new kind of South. And it showed that the South, just as the other sections, was alert to the requirements of the new age America was about to enter.

That was not the only respect in which the South resembled the rest of the country. In many ways its social and economic structure was identical with that of the Northern sections. The ownership of property was widely distributed—70 to 80 per cent of the farmers, the most numerous class, owned their land—and suffrage rested on a popular basis. Southerners generally subscribed to a belief in democracy and practiced democratic politics, although some of their leaders would have curbed majority rule on the national level. (Years before, Calhoun had suggested amending the Constitution to provide for two Presidents, one from the North and one from the South, each with the power to veto acts of Congress.) Southerners also adhered to the set of principles that constituted the American faith—the higher nature of man, the existence of a divine law, the sacred nature of the Constitution— although being the most conservative Americans they had some doubts about

Cyrus Field, one of the nation's greatest industrialists, retired from paper manufacturing at 33 to lay the first Atlantic cable. His success in 1858 was greeted so wildly in New York that the City Hall was set afire—but his cable failed after only three weeks. It was not until 1866 that Field laid the first permanent cable, shown below being unreeled in the hold of the ship.

the doctrine of man's limitless progress, subscribed to so enthusiastically by most of their countrymen.

Class organization in the South often seemed feudal, although the concentration of wealth was no greater than in the Northeast. There was a ruling hierarchy—the great planters, men who owned 20 or more slaves, some 46,000 in number by 1860—but their political position and power eclipsed only slightly that of the Eastern mill masters. The South's agricultural economy differed from the Northwest's in only two respects—it contained large landed units, the plantations, as well as small farms and it produced crops for export abroad, to England and northwestern Europe.

And yet undeniably the South was different. Its people spoke more softly and moved more slowly than their neighbors in the harsher Northern climes. They loved their land with a mystic attachment—in no other section would such a phrase as "our Southland" be employed—and they cherished the ideals of a landed society. Land was the highest form of property ownership, and the more land a man owned the higher his social status. Every man aspired to be a planter, and the planters presided over society much in the fashion of the English country gentry. In no other section were class distinctions so frankly recognized or the position of the ruling hierarchy so openly admitted. Southerners were more convivial and more conservative than Northerners and both for the same reason. The luxuriant environment supported life easily, tempting men to exploit life's pleasures, and just as easily it beat down the material works of men, inducing an amiable acceptance of the inevitable and tempering the conviction—so common among other Americans—that men could conquer their surroundings.

THESE things that were different about the South were the result of geography and climate and historical heritage, and they were significant. But in themselves they were not enough to have set the South apart from the rest of the nation. They alone would not have sparked the flames of sectional controversy or brought the country finally to civil war. Nor would the South's own consciousness of its status—its minority complex, its loss of political equality, its economic grievance, real or fancied, as a producer of raw materials and consumer of finished goods—have led to these ends.

There was one more divisive factor, one more Southern difference, and this one was decisive. It drew into itself all the other variances and dramatized them to a point at which they became unbearable. This factor was, of course, slavery.

Slavery was the only institution that made the South really distinctive, that separated it from the mainstream of American life. Even though the number of slaveholders was small—347,000, or one family out of every four, in 1850—and few of these owned very many bondsmen, slavery permeated every part of Southern life and thought. As a symbol of sectional difference, it came to occupy men's minds everywhere. It aroused all kinds of reactions—aggressive attack and belligerent defense, anger and suspicion and dogmatism and granite inflexibility. It introduced an abstract issue into politics. It was so controversial that it overshadowed the forces of unity in American society—the bonds of history and language and culture and the mechanistic instrumentalities of technology. Terribly compelling and darkly menacing, it loomed behind every political campaign and every political debate in the fateful '50s.

Early railroads, like the Louisville and Nashville line (below), enriched many of their promoters. One of the railroad millionaires was Cornelius Vanderbilt (above). A fierce competitor, he once wrote some associates, "I won't sue you, for the law is too slow. I'll ruin you." The richest man in America, he died gasping the hymn "Come Ye Sinners, Poor and Needy."

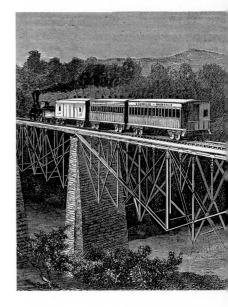

In Bingham's studio profitable portraits outnumber the scenes that later gave him fame.

One man's mid-century America

URING the bustling decades of the middle 1800s, well-to-do folk in Missouri flocked to the studio *(above)* of George Caleb Bingham to have their portraits painted. Bingham was fast and fashionable, and he could be counted on to capture a good likeness of his subjects. Yet the artist's greatest portrait was not of a person at all. Instead it was a fond, homely likeness of life as it was lived in mid-century Missouri—the ebb and flow of traffic along the great river which gave the state its name, the pastimes and political shenanigans of everyday people wherever Bingham found them.

Roaming the countryside with pencil and sketchbook, the artist recorded hundreds of local happenings and characters. These jottings he later worked up in oils, producing busy, bright-hued scenes like the one opposite. Academy art in Bingham's time was inflated with romanticism and sentimentality. But the self-taught Missourian, like many regional American artists after him, was a realist who objectively depicted everything from drunks and demagogues to flea-bitten dogs. Bingham's work reflects more than his own state and people. His paintings form a kind of national album in which a now mature nation will always be able to see again one brief summer moment of its youth.

VOTING DAY, recorded by Bingham in 1852, is a spectacle of vast disorder. As dogs and citizens swarm around the county courthouse, a man in a red shirt is sworn by the judge. Below him a fawning top-hatted politician makes a final plea. At far left a voter who has prepared for his task by imbibing Missouri white mule is dragged to the polls by a helpful party worker.

TAKING TIME OUT, rivermen watch a card game being played by a leering young fellow wearing a broad hat (*left*) and a perplexed old-timer who is trying to decide what card to play. They are enjoying three up, a river game which has now vanished.

A WAIT FOR A CUSTOMER provides a reflective moment for the crew of a woodboat moored along the river. The boats met wood-burning steamboats and sold them fuel—for $3 a cord.

A DANCE ON DECK is performed by a flatboat crewman to the tune of a fiddle and frying pan. This was a common sight, visible, one man said, on almost every boat tied up on the river.

For the toilers of the river, time out for relaxation

IN the 1850s Missouri was becoming the proud cross-roads of the country. The railroad, slowly unwinding westward, reached St. Louis toward the decade's end. Nearby, the currents of the Missouri and the Mississippi coiled together, to be joined a short way downstream by the Ohio. For the people of Bingham's time this 5,000-mile network of rivers provided not only life-giving contact with more than a third of America, but a romantic passageway—south to Frenchified New Orleans, northwest to the wilds of the Rocky Mountain country, northeast toward the throbbing cities of the effete East.

A small-town newspaper, finding no brag big enough for the Missouri, simply called it "the deepest, the shallowest, the bar-iest, the snaggiest, the sandiest, the catfishiest, the swiftest . . . the uncertainest river in all the world." On this waterway rivermen led a life of extremes —"in turn extremely indolent and extremely laborious," sometimes peaceful, sometimes hazardous. What fascinated Bingham were the tranquil moments—simple raftmen playing cards, wood peddlers resting on a bank, gypsylike Creole flatboatmen jigging to a shrill fiddle as their clumsy craft slid south between rolling hills.

Woodsmen on the water

Homeward bound, two fur trappers in a deep-riding pirogue glide down the misty Missouri in one of Bingham's earliest and most magical scenes. The youth amidships is leaning on a blanket which probably hides supplies—and perhaps the winter's take of furs. The animal tethered in the bow is a bear cub.

22

The artist must have seen many a grizzled woodsman on the river like the man at right; the back country of his childhood was full of such roughhewn figures. Between 1807 and 1847 the fur trade earned almost $300,000 a year, but it had obviously begun to peter out. As early as 1840 things were so bad in the wilderness that one trapper complained: "Lizards grow poor, and wolves lean against the sand banks to howl." But oldtimers recalled the good days nostalgically. "No portage was ever too long for me," one Creole *voyageur* reminisced. "Fifty songs could I sing. There is no life so happy."

23

Farmers try their shooting skill for a prize beef which waits at left. These are finalists in a long afternoon's contest, with the target a nail

In the back country, bullets, ballots and braves

Away from the river towns, Missouri was a raw frontier region. Its people, mostly backwoods farmers and traders, were not much for culture. They had to invent their own diversions, like the shooting contest above. Tough and independent, they had a boastful notion that Western life was special. George Bingham, who divided his youth between the Bingham farm and the family tavern in Franklin, knew Missourians well enough to go into politics and get elected to a term in the state legislature. Besides familiarizing him with the give-and-take of vote getting *(top, right)*, his campaigning brought him into contact with all sorts of people, who wound up as studies in the artist's sketch pads.

in a board 40 yards away. Five winners usually shared the prize.

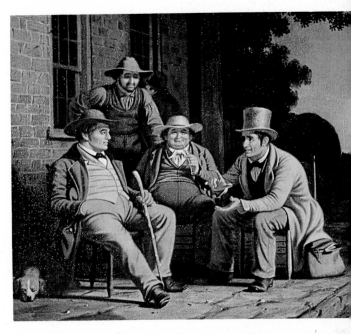

A POLITICAL PITCHMAN in sleek top hat earnestly solicits votes as he tries to charm unimpressed local figures before a rural hotel. To judge from his horse and satchel, he is probably "on the road," a campaign chore that Bingham performed more than once as a candidate.

A LURKING BRAVE painted by Bingham provides a romanticized depiction of a marauding Indian (the artist had probably never met a really hostile one) against the completely realistic background of the Missouri River bluffs that Bingham knew so well.

ROUGH SQUATTERS in front of their ragged log cabin are people who simply cleared public land and began housekeeping. Under an 1841 law squatters got first chance to buy the land. But most of them moved on after a while, lonesome for the wilderness.

A "Stump Orator" reborn

Traveling about during his election campaign, painter-politico Bingham made scores of sketches from which he later created a large, busy painting called *The Stump Orator*. The picture was greeted with great enthusiasm by Missouri newspapers. It was sent east for exhibition, raffled off in 1848 to a citizen

of Savannah, Georgia—and has been missing ever since. But the sketches are today preserved in the St. Louis Mercantile Library. Some of them are arranged here much as Bingham must have placed them, judging from a description that appeared in the *Missouri Republican:* the portly orator, "evidently well pleased with the impression he is making"; his listeners at right "some pleased, some displeased, and some without any idea at all of what he is saying"; and behind him, his opponent, angrily whittling on a stick; a leading citizen in a half-doze; and *(top left)* a busy reporter taking it all down for posterity.

"VERDICT OF THE PEOPLE" is the satiric title chosen by the artist for this political scene —a street corner at the precise moment when election results are being announced to elated victors, grim losers and rowdy bystanders. Bingham wrote of man's political behavior: "God help poor human nature." But he stayed in politics—and he continued to portray human nature more enthusiastically than any other artist of his time.

2. THE DESPERATE COMPROMISE

THE 31st Congress convened on December 3, 1849, in an atmosphere of tense expectancy. On the surface it was just another session, a new Congress meeting to organize under a new President. But below the surface, behind the jocular greetings, the backslapping, the cloakroom negotiations and the other manifestations of an American legislative body about to begin its labors, there was something else, something ominous and curiously unpolitical.

Georgia's Alexander H. Stephens, 90 pounds of frail flesh and brilliant brain, that "queer looking bundle" who once said his idea of happiness was to be warm, reported the feelings of the Southern Whigs: "I find the feeling among Southern members for a dissolution of the Union—if anti-slavery should be pressed to extremity—is becoming much more general. . . . Men are now beginning to talk of it seriously, who, twelve months ago, hardly permitted themselves to think of it." New York's saturnine William H. Seward announced the sentiments of the Northern Whigs. "The malcontents of the South mean to be factious and . . . expect to compel 'a compromise,'" he told an intimate. But Zachary Taylor was willing to try conclusions with them and to face them down as Andrew Jackson had the nullifiers back in the 1830s; "the President," said Seward with satisfaction, ". . . will not flinch from any duty." So said two sectional spokesmen of the Whigs, which had once boasted of being the party of moderation and conciliation. Grim old John C. Calhoun of South Carolina, who thought that the time for compromise had long passed, permitted himself

APOSTLE OF CONCESSION Millard Fillmore, who urged the Compromise of 1850 to help save the Union, stands before a Washington scene dominated by the distant Capitol.

31

an expression of hope for his section: "The South is more united than I ever knew it to be, and more bold and decided. The North must give way, or there will be a rupture."

These were the voices that were heard—hard, angry and unyielding. Men who believed in compromise and who dreaded a split were oppressed and for the moment muted.

Almost immediately the tensed emotions exploded into action. In the House of Representatives, which had to elect its Speaker before organizing, the Democrats and the Whigs were approximately equal in number. The balance of power lay with a handful of Free-Soilers, a third party opposed to any extension of slavery to the new territories of California and New Mexico that had come into being in 1848. The Whigs renominated for Speaker the dignified Robert C. Winthrop of Massachusetts; the Democrats put forward the moderate Southerner Howell Cobb, a rotund Georgia planter. With the parties so evenly divided, neither candidate could muster a majority. The balloting continued day after day, and then week after week, while the atmosphere grew more and more rancorous. The Democrats, seeking to center their strength on somebody who could command both Northern and Southern support, shifted their votes to Indiana's William J. Brown, whose voting record indicated a sympathy for Southern views. Brown was forging ahead when it was disclosed that he had pledged important committee assignments to antislavery men. Pandemonium broke out on the floor and the House had to be adjourned. The next day a Northern member hurled the word "disunionist" at a Southerner, and a physical collision between the two angry men was barely prevented.

Suddenly amid the din, up towered huge and hearty Robert Toombs of Georgia. He had as much attachment for the Union as any man, he bellowed in his bull voice. But "I do not . . . hesitate to avow before this House and the Country, and in the presence of the living God, that if by your legislation you seek to drive us from the territories of California and New Mexico . . . and to abolish slavery in this District, thereby attempting to fix a national degradation upon half the states of this Confederacy, *I am for disunion*." Toombs's blunt warning apparently had a sobering effect, for two days before Christmas the House named Cobb Speaker by a simple plurality vote. It had taken three weeks and 63 ballots to reach the decision.

I N the Senate, with its more stable composition, there was no trouble over organization. But the voices there were no less strident, and every mention of slavery brought forth cries of wrath. When resolutions were presented from Vermont's legislature condemning slavery, the Southern members broke out with wild denunciations. Replying for the North, Ohio's Salmon P. Chase, portly and pompous, declared that "no menace of disunion . . . will move us from the path which in our judgment it is due to ourselves and the people whom we represent to pursue."

What issues had brought the union of American states to this condition in which men could seriously argue the merits of disunion? Toombs had stated most of them in his House speech. As a result of the war with Mexico in 1846 the United States had acquired an imperial domain of over half a million square miles. Should slavery be excluded from the new area or permitted to expand into it? There was complete agreement on one point: A *state* could decide the status of slavery within its bounds in any way it wished. The

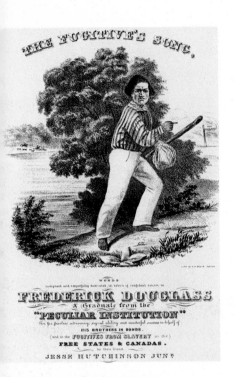

Family singing groups were popular in the 1850s. One, the Hutchinsons, who sang for temperance and other worthy causes, saluted runaway slave Frederick Douglass, "a graduate from the 'Peculiar Institution,'" in this song. Douglass, a slave until he was 21, became minister to Haiti in 1889.

disagreement concerned who should determine that status during the territorial period before statehood.

In the debate that raged throughout 1849, four formulas were advanced. The advocates of the first formula, the Wilmot Proviso, originally submitted in 1846, had a ready answer: Congress should control—and Congress should exclude slavery from the new lands. The national legislature had the legal authority to make regulations for the national territories, they argued, and it had a moral duty to reserve these lands for freedom. The Proviso proposal represented the most extreme Northern position. The second formula also represented an extreme sectional position, that of the most fiery Southerners. It was as starkly simple as the Proviso solution: slaves were property, the territories were the joint possession of the states, and Southerners could emigrate to the new lands with their human property just as other people could with other property. The third formula proposed to end the controversy by extending the Missouri Compromise line of 36° 30′ westward through the new territories to the Pacific Ocean, with slavery banned north of the line but permitted south of it. It appealed to moderates in the South but generated little support outside that section. But another compromise proposal did attract moderates in both sections. This, the fourth formula, was known as popular sovereignty, and much would be heard about it in the future.

A Southern aristocrat, Georgia's Howell Cobb, who hid three chins and a kindly nature behind a flowing beard, owned 1,000 slaves. But in 1849 he was still ardently for the Union and many Southerners supported him reluctantly in his fight with Robert Winthrop for the speakership of the House.

THE doctrine of popular sovereignty—or "squatter sovereignty," as it was sometimes contemptuously referred to—was peculiarly the property of the Northwestern Democrats, and it was advocated most loudly by the man who was emerging as their leader, Stephen A. Douglas, senator from Illinois. Squat in figure—he barely topped five feet—large of head and mighty of voice, Douglas was known to some as the "Little Giant" of the prairies, to others as that "steam engine in britches." He was an unusually adroit manipulator, but he—and other Western politicans as well—faced a problem that challenged the ablest talents. Their constituents wanted to keep slavery out of the territories, and the party chiefs had to provide an assurance that it would be banned. But the leaders also desired to win national elections—Douglas, in particular, hoped to be President—and this meant that the party had to be held together as a national organization, that the Southern wing must not be goaded into withdrawing. Popular sovereignty was a subtle doctrine conceived to satisfy both sections. It proposed that Congress should neither exclude slavery nor encourage its expansion. Instead, the status of the institution would be decided by the people of each territory through their territorial legislature.

At first glance this was an alluring proposal. Popular sovereignty tempted Southerners because it avoided the slap in the face of the Wilmot Proviso and held out the possibility that the South might win some of the territories. At the same time it could be presented to the Northern voters for what it actually was—an exclusionist device. For in any competition depending on numbers the North was certain to win. But, as would eventually become apparent, the doctrine contained certain weaknesses—not the least of which was that it ignored completely the morality of the slavery question.

All the proposed formulas were discussed in the 1849 debate over slavery in the territories, but each of them was eventually pushed into the background. Indeed, as the dispute continued, it swelled in volume and asperity and widened in scope. Human bondage itself became an issue. Some ardent

A Northern aristocrat, Robert C. Winthrop, who came from a family of colonial governors, educators and scientists, was as much out of step with his followers as Cobb was. For want of sufficient antislavery fervor Winthrop lost not only the speakership, but later election to the Senate as well.

Northerners declared that the existence of slavery in the national capital was a disgrace and demanded that at least the trade in slaves be abolished there. Some Southerners denounced the "personal liberty laws" of Northern states, which hampered the capture of runaway slaves and, overlooking for the moment the South's devotion to states' rights, demanded a drastic national fugitive slave law. A Texas territorial demand was brought up: the Lone Star State was claiming for itself a huge area of land east of the Rio Grande which the United States was claiming on behalf of the territory of New Mexico. Southerners supported the larger boundary for Texas; Northerners opposed it. As an intriguing side issue, the holders of Texas bonds, many of whom were non-Texans, pressed the national government to assume that state's debt—and urged Texas in return to accept a reduced land area.

Hanging over all these questions was the same hard fact that had been at issue almost 30 years before in the debate over Missouri statehood: the country's sectional balance was relentlessly shifting. The South, its proportion of the total population dropping every decade, was a minority in the House of Representatives and in the Electoral College. Only in the Senate—where the number of slave and free states had remained equal ever since the Missouri Compromise of 1820 (it now stood at 15 to 15)—did the South retain, in effect, a veto. If the territory acquired from Mexico was to be organized against slavery and eventually to come into the Union as two or more free states, the last rampart would go down; and the South would, in the words of an Alabaman, enter upon the condition of "a fixed, dreary, hopeless minority."

The steely glance from under Daniel Webster's top hat in this engraving, taken from a photograph, is that of a politician saying "No." When the photographer asked him to pose for a "first" picture, Webster growled: "Your first will be your last." He held still for the 11-second exposure and departed.

WHEN General Zachary Taylor, the Whig victor in the election of 1848, assumed the presidency in March 1849, no decision had been reached on the status of slavery in the Mexican cession lands. The vast area was still being administered by military officials as the territories of California and New Mexico. Ordinarily the absence of civil government would have meant little to the few inhabitants of the region, but the discovery of gold in 1848 had dramatically changed the picture in California. People poured into the area, and by the end of 1849 California boasted a population of 100,000, well above the minimum for statehood. To the soldier mind of President Taylor the miracle of the gold rush presented a perfect way out of the developing political crisis. Everybody conceded that a state entering the Union—unlike a territory seeking self-government—could do as it wished about slavery. Therefore Taylor decided the thing for him to do was to encourage California and also New Mexico to apply for statehood without going through a territorial-government phase. Then the whole ugly problem would be settled.

It mattered not at all to the President that both territories would undoubtedly choose to come in as free states. Taylor was a Louisiana slaveholder, but he was also a soldier who had served all over the country, and his outlook was national rather than sectional. He had had no experience with political situations, and he had little patience with their complexity. He preferred the direct approach and the simple solution. "Old Zack is a good old soul," observed Horace Greeley, "but don't know himself from a side of sole leather in the way of statesmanship."

Old, gaunt and garbed in black, Henry Clay came quavering back to the Senate in 1849 after a seven-year absence. He was, he said, "exhausted," and intended to "be a calm and quiet looker-on." But the old urge to leadership shortly emerged and he was engaged in arranging the Compromise of 1850.

Taylor sent out agents to prod the two territories to action. California, eager for civil government, acted quickly, and by October of 1849 had prepared a constitution prohibiting slavery and was ready to become a state.

New Mexico proceeded with more deliberation, but it too was receptive to statehood and set the machinery for entrance into motion.

The country had watched the old soldier's abrupt handling of the situation with some astonishment. Southerners were aghast. Suddenly the choicest parts of the new territory were about to be snatched from them—and what was unpardonable, by one of their own. In strict logic they could not deny what they had always admitted, that a state could exclude slavery. But they could and did deny that California or New Mexico really desired statehood. Both had been pressured into asking for it, cried even moderate Southerners. More extreme ones charged that the President, dominated by such Northern zealots as Seward, wanted to deprive the South of all rights in the territories. From Southerners in Congress came such bitter phrases as "gross injustice," "an excess of power," "executive tyranny" and "gross usurpation of powers."

Even responsible Southern leaders acknowledged the possibility of secession if California was admitted, and from Mississippi came a call for a Southern convention to meet in Nashville in June 1850, to consider what action should be taken to resist Northern "aggressions." As excitement mounted in the South, it rose also in the North. There men declared that if the other section wanted a trial of strength they were ready. "The North is determined that slavery shall not pollute the soil of lands now free . . . even if it should come to a dissolution of the Union," proclaimed one Ohio newspaper. This was the situation that faced Congress in the last month of 1849—a country convulsed by bitter controversy, an apprehensive and apparently adamant South, and an aroused and equally stubborn North. It was a situation to challenge the ablest political minds the 31st Congress could offer.

That Congress contained, especially in the Senate, a long cast of notables. Heading the list were three great men who had begun their parliamentary careers before or during the War of 1812—Henry Clay of Kentucky, John C. Calhoun of South Carolina and Daniel Webster of Massachusetts. They were feeble now and in their twilight. But they could still stir men's minds with words, and their presence evoked memories of a glorious past. There too from another era, the era of Andrew Jackson, were Thomas Hart Benton of Missouri, rugged in figure and rough of speech, and Sam Houston of Texas, sparkling in his panther-skin waistcoat. Forging to the front were the younger leaders, the men who would dominate the political scene in the years ahead —Seward and Chase and Douglas from the North, and Stephens, Toombs and Jefferson Davis of Mississippi from the South.

Another of the Great Triumvirate to engage in the 1850 debate was John C. Calhoun. Calhoun was desperately ill—but when Webster expressed regret one day that his old foe could not be present he laboriously stood erect and gasped triumphantly: "The Senator from South Carolina is in his seat!"

THESE were all able and experienced politicians, and most of them doubted that Taylor's simple statehood formula could solve the current crisis. As had become clear in the course of the debate, the country was afflicted—in Clay's words—with five bleeding wounds: California, the territories, the Texas boundary, fugitive slaves and the slave trade in the District of Columbia. All were now inextricably intermingled—but the President could see only one of them.

The new year broke amidst expressions of ill will and unhappy predictions. On the floor of the Senate, Jefferson Davis, slight, intense and intellectual, looking very much like a younger Calhoun, rose to speak. He warned grimly that the people of his state would know how to meet an attack on their rights. "They well know how to sustain the institutions which they inherited, even by civil war, if that be provoked," he trumpeted. "They will march up to the issue and meet it face to face."

With tempers mounting and threats multiplying, the moderate men of both sections decided that at last the time had come when they must act. By common consent, they turned to Henry Clay. The slender, graceful, magnetic Kentuckian was a sick man with but two years to live. Yet his superb voice rang out as clearly as when he had been the young "Harry of the West," and he had lost none of his power to charm the hearts of men and women. Dreading disunion and devoted to the art of accommodation, Clay was quite ready to assume once again the leadership of the forces of compromise.

Guided by the North Star, Harriet Tubman escaped to Canada from slavery in Maryland in 1849. At the risk of her freedom she returned to Maryland again and again to lead out others, including her own aged parents, by way of the Underground Railroad. In the Deep South during the Civil War she served the North as a spy and scout. She died in 1913 at age 90.

ON January 29, Clay presented to the Senate a set of resolutions dealing with all of the "bleeding wounds." He proposed that (1) California should be admitted as a free state; (2) territorial governments should be provided for the rest of the Mexican cession area with no congressional action either for the exclusion or introduction of slavery; (3) Texas should accept a reduced Western boundary and the United States should in exchange assume the Texas debt; (4) the slave trade—though not slavery itself—should be abolished in the District of Columbia; and (5) Congress should enact a law for the effective apprehension of fugitive slaves.

Early in February, Clay supported his resolutions in two eloquent speeches. Thousands came from neighboring cities and towns—Alexandria, Baltimore, Philadelphia—to hear him and sat perspiring in a Senate chamber that had been overheated to 100°. Clay spoke not only as a Whig but as a realist and lover of the Union, and he pleaded with both sections to be moderate. Slavery could never enter the disputed territories, he assured the North. "What more do you want?" he asked. "You have got what is worth more than a thousand Wilmot Provisos. You have nature on your side—facts upon your side—and this truth staring you in the face, that there is no slavery in those territories." Addressing himself to the proslavery forces, he declared that Southern rights were safer in the Union than they would be outside it, and that secession would inevitably be followed by war, "furious . . . bloody . . . implacable" war. The apparently frail old man seemed to gather strength from the great occasion. He flung out his words to the far reaches of the chamber and to the galleries, and when he finished women rushed forward to plant kisses on his face.

The first plea for conciliation and compromise had been made, and it was answered immediately by the voices of Southern extremism. Jefferson Davis reduced the issue to terms terrible in their simplicity. The North meant to conquer the minority section, he cried, and the South could only submit or fight. But the true voice of the unyielding South came, as everybody knew it would, from the senator who for long years had said it was fruitless to yield, the "cast-iron man," that brooding and metaphysical mind, John C. Calhoun.

In the last stages of tuberculosis, Calhoun had less than a month to live when on March 4 he sat swathed in flannels, his face impassive and his eyes heavy-lidded, and heard a colleague read his speech. In it he ignored Clay's resolutions. Instead he discussed what was for him the larger and the only issue, the security of the minority South in the Union. Only the stronger section could prevent a dissolution of the nation—by conceding to the South equal rights in the territories, by observing its obligation to return fugitive slaves, by ceasing to agitate against slavery and by agreeing to some amendment to the Constitution giving the minority section a power of veto. If the North would not do these things, then let the sections part in peace, the speech concluded. "If you are unwilling we should part in peace tell us so, and we shall know what to do, when you reduce the question to submission or resistance." The dying man had called for no surrender by the South and complete surrender by the North.

But on March 7 another voice for moderation sounded in the Senate, and this was a famous and powerful voice, perhaps the most compelling among the orators of the time. Daniel Webster, the "Godlike Daniel," with bulging brow and mastiff mouth and attired in his ceremonial suit of Revolutionary blue and buff, arose to make his last great forensic effort. Like Clay, he had but two years to live, and he chose, as Clay had, to speak not as a Whig alone but as a nationalist too. He deliberately addressed his main appeal to his own North, to the conservative elements there that could be swayed to compromise. There was no need for a law to exclude slavery from the territories, he argued. Slavery would not go where it would not be profitable; it was already barred by the facts of geography and economics. "I would not take pains to reaffirm an ordinance of nature, nor to reenact the will of God. And I would put in no Wilmot Proviso, for the purpose of a taunt or a reproach." In his zeal to conciliate, Webster even reproved the abolitionists for their intemperate language and—knowing full well it would arouse violent dissent in his native New England—denounced the personal liberty laws of the Northern states that prevented the apprehension of runaway slaves.

The dissent he expected was not long in coming. To a man, the antislavery intellectuals and writers cast him from the fold. "So fallen! So lost!" lamented John Greenleaf Whittier. And Longfellow echoed: "Fallen, fallen, fallen from his high estate." The most scathing indictment came from Ralph Waldo Emerson. Webster claimed to be a moral man, said Emerson, but he added in a terrible sentence of summary: "All the drops of his blood have eyes that look downward." He went on: "It is neither praise nor blame to say that he has no moral perception, no moral sentiment, but in that region—to use the phrase of the phrenologists—a hole in the head. . . . He has no faith in the power of self-government. . . . In Massachusetts, in 1776, he would, beyond all question, have been a refugee." The Concord philosopher later added a caustic couplet to this attack on his state's senator: "Why did all manly gifts in Webster fail? He wrote on Nature's grandest brow, *For Sale.*"

F OUR days after Webster's speech another Northern Whig took the floor to reply to him and to state the extreme antislavery view. Slight in stature, with a small, pointed face, William H. Seward looked more like a boy than the veteran politician he was. He drew the issues as squarely as Calhoun had. California must be admitted without conditions. Slavery must be excluded from the territories. He would accept no compromise because he believed "all legislative compromises radically wrong and essentially vicious. They involve the surrender of the exercise of judgment and conscience." And if all this were not enough to infuriate Southerners, Seward went on to declare that the Constitution was not the supreme guide for the government of the territories—there was a higher law, the law of God, that demanded the national lands be dedicated to freedom.

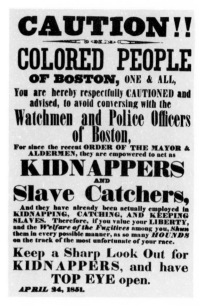

Bitter Bostonians posted placards such as this one around their city. Written by abolitionist Theodore Parker, it warns blacks to beware of the city police, who, under the Fugitive Slave Act, received fees for returning runaway slaves. As time passed, many Northern police refused to detain blacks—and some Northern states threatened to punish those who did.

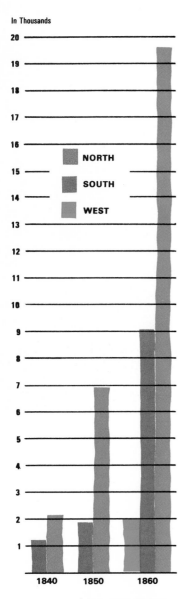

In Thousands

20
19
18
17
16
15
14
13
12
11
10
9
8
7
6
5
4
3
2
1

NORTH

SOUTH

WEST

1840   1850   1860

U.S. RAILROADS:
TWO DECADES OF GROWTH

From 1840 to 1860, U.S. railroads expanded at a dizzying rate: from 3,300 to over 30,000 miles of track. The greatest progress was in the North (blue)—a fact of vital importance in the Civil War. In 1850 the South (gray) had only one third the North's trackage. Though the proportion was reduced in the next 10 years, the actual gap grew greater: on the eve of war, there were 9,000 miles of track in the South, nearly 20,000 in the North. Meanwhile the first rail growth appeared west of the Mississippi, looking toward 1869, when the first transcontinental line would be laid.

This was stiff language, and Seward explained candidly why he was using it. He was convinced, he said, that the Southern threat to secede was a bluff and that the Southerners would back down if confronted by a determined North. This might seem to be gambling the nation's fate on a dubious guess, but it was a chance many in the free states were apparently ready to risk.

Clay's resolutions had been referred to a Select Committee of Thirteen headed by the Kentuckian. Early in May, acting for the committee, Clay presented a report which was immediately embodied in three bills substantially reflecting his proposals of January 29. Supporting the bills, Clay spoke with his usual eloquence. If the committee's measures could be submitted to a popular vote, he affirmed, they would be endorsed by nine tenths of the people.

There was some exaggeration in Clay's analysis but not much. Public opinion in all parts of the country was shifting in favor of compromise. The whole country was about to enter on a period of prosperity and expansion that demanded calm in place of crisis. But the sentiment for concession did not immediately penetrate to Congress. The first of the committee's measures failed on several votes, and as the heat of early summer bore down on Washington the passage of any kind of compromise seemed as remote as ever.

There were still strong influences working against a settlement. President Taylor continued to insist that California must be admitted without any conditions attached. The old soldier's fighting blood was aroused: if the South thought it could blackmail the government with a threat of secession, let the test come and see who was the stronger party! Most Northern Whigs upheld his stand. Another factor stalling action was Clay's poor parliamentary procedure. He offended some Senators by maintaining that several elements of the compromise must be approved or rejected in a single bill, and he talked too much—between February and August he spoke more than 70 times.

THEN, fatefully, the personal obstacles to compromise began to disappear. Calhoun died on March 31. His departure left the Southern extremists without a leader, and moderate Southerners said it was God's interposition to save the country. On July 4, President Taylor overly exerted himself at ceremonies at the still-unfinished Washington Monument, ate and drank too much, and died of a violent stomach inflammation. Moderate Northerners said that if he had lived the sections would have come to war.

Into the first office from the vice presidency moved the handsome but colorless Millard Fillmore of New York, who believed in compromise. Immediately the new President threw his influence behind the adjustment measures, and some Northern Whigs fell in line behind him. Finally Clay, exhausted by his long labors, left for Newport, Rhode Island, to rest in the sea breezes, and Stephen A. Douglas took over the leadership of the compromise forces.

The Little Giant proved to be a masterful political craftsman. First he broke the Compromise into parts and offered each item separately. Then, staying in the background and speaking rarely, he manipulated the combinations required to put the bills through. By mid-September he had steered to passage the set of measures Americans would come to call the Compromise of 1850.

In final form this Compromise resembled Clay's original resolutions and the report of the Committee of Thirteen, and yet it differed in minor detail from both. California was admitted as a free state. New Mexico and Utah were organized as territories with no congressional exclusion of slavery. All territorial laws were to be submitted to Congress for approval or rejection. The terminology of this section was made deliberately ambiguous to garner votes, but it was obviously intended to apply Douglas' pet formula of popular sovereignty to both territories. Texas was to relinquish its claim to part of New Mexico and to receive from the national government a payment of $10 million. The slave trade was abolished in the District of Columbia. Finally, the new Fugitive Slave Act placed the full power of the national government behind the apprehension of runaway slaves.

IN many ways, the Fugitive Slave Act was the most significant element of the Compromise. By insisting on including it, the South committed a serious political error. Its harsh provisions affronted Northern moral sensibilities. It repelled the most moderate Northerners, those who were otherwise disposed to view the South's case sympathetically. Moreover, it put the South, the advocate of the largest possible exercise of state powers, in the anomalous position of forcing the bluntest kind of national intervention in state affairs. In any event, there was little practical need for such a law. The number of escaping slaves was small, probably averaging no more than a thousand a year. The number of these who reached the North was even smaller—and most of them came from the border states. The real reason behind the Southern demand for the law was its importance as a symbol.

The Compromise of 1850, like most compromises, had settled much and little. On balance, it gave slightly more to the North, which got California and the promise of New Mexico and Utah. But these gains only registered legally what was certain to come anyway. California's admission could not have been indefinitely delayed by any Southern opposition, and the remaining territories were clearly unsuited for slavery. The South had won concessions that were more abstract than real—the right in theory and law to carry slaves to the territories and a meaningless measure to catch a few fugitive slaves. Inevitably and irresistibly, the balance of sectional power was swinging against the South. This was a fact no enactment of Congress could halt.

For the moment the men who made the Compromise had averted a crisis that might well have led to disunion and war. If war had come in 1850—as it might have if the Compromise had not been proposed in time—the North, with its railroad and industrial system still in process of development, would not have been as well prepared as it would be a decade later. But in 1850 the Southern people were not as united or resolved as they would be in that other decade. Their devotion to the Union, to its spiritual concept and its material advantage, had been shaken, but it was not yet shattered. If there had been no Compromise proposal, some of the Southern states would certainly have seceded, but some would have remained and some would have hesitated. President Taylor would have responded with a show of force that just possibly might have divided the South and ended right there the ideal of state sovereignty and the hazard of national division. Then there would have been no American Civil War.

But these were contingencies that the men of 1850 as patriotic Americans could not envision or consider. They knew only that the nation was threatened, and they had acted as best they could to save it. They thought they had won a peace. Only time would reveal that the great Compromise was merely an uneasy truce.

Missouri's Thomas Hart Benton, whose fiery egotism was once called a "national institution in which every patriotic American could take a just pride," argued for peace in the 1850s. In rolling periods he cried: "I say, in brief and in short, that the two halves of this Union . . . were made for each other as much as Adam and Eve were made for each other."

In a scrimshaw scene carved on the tooth of a whale, a ship's four whaleboats give chase to their quarry.

A flourishing industry on the sea

IN 1712 a fierce north wind unexpectedly opened the way to a great new American industry. That year a sloop out of Nantucket, hunting the shore-hugging right whale, was blown off its usual hunting grounds by a sudden gale from the north. Far out in the Atlantic, Captain Christopher Hussey sighted the first school of sperm whales he had ever seen. A catch was made and brought back to port. Hussey's find transformed whaling in America.

Sperm whales turned out to be more difficult to find and hunt than right whales; furthermore, they attacked as fiercely as they were attacked *(opposite)*, and they roamed far out to sea. But they repaid the dangers of the chase. Their oil shone brighter in lamps than right-whale oil did, and there was treasure in a sperm whale's head—spermaceti, five tons of it, from which could be made the finest candles ever known. By 1846, some 736 American whaling ships, ranging the seven seas, were bringing back an average annual catch worth eight million dollars, and sailors were recording the flourishing industry in whalebone and ivory carvings called scrimshaw *(above)*.

By the 1860s, however, the fleet began to encounter difficulty. Petroleum oil, first produced in quantity in 1859, began to replace whale oil in homes and factories. During the Civil War 70 whalers were sunk by the Confederates. The crushing blow came in 1871, when a great fleet of Arctic whalers was wrecked by ice brought by an unexpected southwest wind. Thus the industry that was founded by a good wind was sped toward oblivion by an ill one.

AN ATTACKING WHALE smashes a boat. One whale, a ship's log of 1754 recorded, "stove ye boat & . . . killed the midshipman . . . outwright a Sad & Awful Providence."

A harpooned whale takes a boat for a "Nantucket sleigh ride." At such times, speeds of 20 knots were not uncommon and a seaman who

Abundant stores to sustain a perilous profession

WHALERS' SUPPLIES crowd a New London wharf as two ships are fitted out for the season's hunting. Almost everything below decks was stored in casks: food, water, coal for the stoves—and, with luck, 80,000 gallons of oil on the return trip.

B Y 1791, the whalers were ranging around the Horn and into the Pacific, and by 1848, into the Arctic. Ships had to be provisioned for voyages of three years or more. (One New London vessel actually stayed out 11 years before returning with a full load; it picked up supplies at Pacific islands.) In the great whaling towns, ships' outfitters were constantly at work, and bakers baked thousands of loaves for the long voyages. Each ship became a giant store containing "spare boats, spare spars . . . and spare everything, almost, but a spare Captain and a duplicate ship," Herman Melville wrote. It was all needed. One log of 1838 noted: "In four whales we have lost 22 irons, 1 lance." There were also greater losses. Boats were "stove in" frequently, and sometimes the ships themselves were attacked by whales. One, the *Essex*, was sunk in the Pacific by a raging 85-foot whale that "came down upon us with full speed and struck the ship with his head." In the vessel's three whaleboats, with little food, 20 men set out for land 3,000 miles away. Eight survived—and five went back to whaling.

A SCRIMSHAW SAILOR, armed with sextant and spyglass, strolls the globe while a fanciful bird of paradise flutters above him. This inscribed carving of a "Yankee tar" was a whalebone corset stay, a sentimental whaler's gift to his love.

got caught in the line might be flipped into the ocean. When the whale tired, the rowers pulled up close and the death blow was struck.

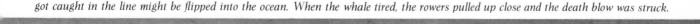

Six men against sixty tons in a fight to the death

WHEN a whale was "raised" by the lookout in the rigging, boats were hastily lowered and the chase began. Five men rowed; an officer called the headsman steered, facing the whale. When the great hump loomed close, the headsman would cry: "Stand up and let him have it solid!" The harpooner would leap up and hurl his iron. Then, in the madly plunging boat, he would change places with the headsman, who made the kill.

With lethal accuracy, a headsman strikes with his lance and "reaches the life" of the whale. A whale might spout blood for an hour,

Up close, sometimes right up on the whale's back, the headsman drove his six-foot lances in, churning them until the whale went into its death flurry. The work was hazardous and difficult, and although the captain might get $1/15$ of the profits and a mate $1/25$, a crewman often got as little as $1/150$. From this was deducted the cost of his outfit and various other incidental expenses. Many a luckless sailor returned home in debt.

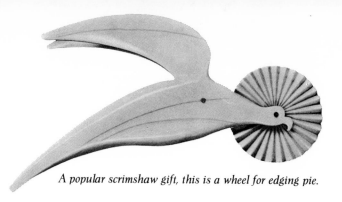

A popular scrimshaw gift, this is a wheel for edging pie.

turning toward the sun to die. In his final savage flurry, his thrashing flukes and snapping jaws frequently dealt death to his killers.

A one-ton "blanket piece" is stripped from a whale. Blanket pieces were cut into "horse pieces" and "Bible leaves," then boiled into oil.

In a busy scene, a fleet of whalers exchanges attacks with a school of whales. One whale is marked with a whaleboat's flag (left); another

Cutting a giant down to size in a floating factory

WHALING was hard work not only during the sea chase but after it, when the home ship became a seaborne oil factory. With the dead whale firmly secured to the vessel's side, cutting stages were lowered (*left*) and the cutting-in began. Winch cables hooked in the blubber unrolled it from the whale, then let it down on deck where the pieces were sliced and "tried-out," or boiled, in huge caldrons. One sperm whale might yield 2,500 gallons of oil—worth $1.49 a gallon in 1854—plus precious spermaceti. The work was messy and back-breaking. Yet in spite of all the toil and trouble of a whaler's life, at the industry's peak as many as 17,000 men, hoping for a full ship and ready for any adventure, served in the greatest whaling fleet on the seas.

A scrimshaw proposal, carved at sea, records a sailor's hopes.

"jaws back," hurling men into the sea; a third splinters a boat with a blow of its flukes; while a fourth (right) receives the coup de grâce.

3. RETURN TO CRISIS

I FERVENTLY hope," said the handsome, slender man on the platform before the Capitol, "that the question is at rest, and that no sectional or ambitious or fanatical excitement may again threaten the durability of our institutions or obscure the light of our prosperity." President Franklin Pierce stood in the cold, raw March air as he delivered his inaugural address in 1853. "We have been carried in safety through a perilous crisis," he continued. "Let the period be remembered as an admonition, and not as an encouragement, in any section of the Union, to make experiments where experiments are fraught with such fearful hazard."

Pierce spoke with conviction, and his words seemed to promise the beginning of an era of sectional peace and national prosperity. The crisis of 1850 was in the past, and its great Compromise insured tranquillity in the future. Most Americans desired calm and not controversy. The '50s opened in a burst of affluence that presaged a new cycle of economic expansion. Men in all sections turned their attention from the rhetoric of politics to the arithmetic of profits—the price of cotton and corn, the dividends of stocks and bonds, and the extension of factories and farms. Trade and commerce were thriving; New England's great clipper ships, famed for their speed and grace, were carrying American cargoes to every part of the world. Amid this boom Americans had little time for serious matters; surveying the pervasive prosperity and noting the passive reaction of the voters to political agitation, antislavery

COURIER OF PROSPERITY, a clipper built by Bostonian Donald McKay heads downwind under full sail. McKay's ships were the swiftest in an age of booming U.S. trade.

leader Charles Francis Adams complained: "The moral tone of the Free States never was more thoroughly broken."

The mood of the country had dominated the election of 1852. Both parties endorsed the Compromise measures and called for a continuation of the comparative calm that had prevailed since their passage. In selecting their candidates, Democrats and Whigs alike passed over leaders who had been recently prominent or who were associated with the late crisis. The Democrats chose Pierce of New Hampshire, who had had a short, obscure political career. The Whigs picked General Winfield Scott, who had had no political career at all.

It was hard to know what significance to read into the result. Possibly because they seemed to stand more strongly for the finality of the Compromise, the Democrats carried the contest. Yet, although Pierce's electoral majority was decisive—27 states and 254 electoral votes to four and 42 for Scott—his popular margin was narrow, only 60,000 more votes than the combined total of Scott and the Free-Soil candidate, John P. Hale. In the close division, there was an intimation that the grand agreement was not so completely accepted as it seemed to be on the surface.

In both North and South, there were people who had never acceded to the Compromise as a good or final settlement. In both there were some men of unyielding principle who from the first were eager to scuttle it. Alabama's silver-tongued orator, William L. Yancey, delivered speech after speech warning that the South had been led into a trap. "All my aims and objects," he admitted, "are to cast before the people of the South as great a mass of wrongs committed on them, injuries and insults that have been done, as I possibly can." And a Georgia editor declared: "There is a feud between North and South which may be smothered, but never overcome."

The Conscience Whigs, the most extreme antislavery political faction in the North, were silent for a period after 1850. With these men there was, for reasons of party, a biting of lips, a disposition to give the adjustment a trial. But in the antislavery group which stood beyond the politicians, the out-and-out abolitionists, there was a sense of outrage and an intensified determination to continue the fight until the inevitable victory was achieved.

William Lloyd Garrison, sincere and single-minded, an Old Testament moralist who for 20 years had contended for emancipation in his *Liberator*, thundered that no act of Congress could stay moral progress or save slavery: "Slavery must be overthrown. . . . No matter, though, to effect it, every party should be torn by dissensions, every sect dashed into fragments, the national compact dissolved, the land filled with the horrors of a civil and a servile war —still, slavery must be buried in the grave of infamy, beyond the possibility of a resurrection." Other abolitionists, in words almost as violent, drummed the same theme—there could be no peace until slavery was put down.

ALTHOUGH the abolitionist attack swelled in volume, it did not reach a mass audience. But in 1852 there occurred the most effective single abolitionist blow at slavery, and it was struck by the gentle hand of a woman. Harriet Beecher Stowe embodied the reforming religious spirit of New England, its lofty moral sense and its terrible zeal. It was bred into her. Her father and five of her six brothers were ministers, and she married a professor of Biblical literature. While living in Cincinnati, she tried her hand at writing and found she had a talent for it. Her whole family was intensely antislavery, and she was

The flamboyantly patriotic appeal of this 1852 campaign banner was of very little help to presidential candidate Winfield Scott and his running mate William Graham. Their Whig cause failed, as was prophesied in a Democratic slogan of the day: "We Polked you in 1844, we shall Pierce you in 1852!"

curious enough about the institution to journey over the Ohio River into Kentucky to observe it. In 1850 she and her husband went to Maine to live. Back in her native section she heard on every hand denunciations of slavery and piteous tales of fugitive slaves, and all her crusading ardor boiled to the surface.

Urged on by her family and her own inclination, she decided to write something about slavery. The result was a serial story in a religious magazine that kept growing until it became a novel. Published under the title *Uncle Tom's Cabin; or, Life Among the Lowly*, it was an instantaneous and sensational success. The first printing sold out in two days, new printings could not keep up with the orders, and by the end of 1852 over 300,000 copies had been sold. Even then the demand did not cease, and dramatized as a play the book reached a still-wider audience. Published abroad, it sold even better—more than one million copies in the British Empire alone.

But its importance was in America. Most people in the North who snapped up the book did not pause to note that along with undoubted literary quality —Mrs. Stowe could write—went some serious shortcomings. The author's frank purpose was to demonstrate the brutal nature of slavery and its brutalizing effect on all people, even good ones, who were associated with it. To that end she created characters who were more stereotypes than real people and manipulated them in situations that were obviously contrived. Even as a straight-out description of the Southern social system, the book contained inaccuracies, as Mrs. Stowe had later to concede.

But these technical defects were unnoticed and unimportant at the moment. What gave the book its tremendous impact was the depiction of slavery in terms of individuals. Heretofore most abolitionists had attacked it as an institution. But here was something much more effective—not sermons or statistics but people, poor Uncle Tom, little Eva, Topsy and cruel Simon Legree. The readers who agonized over their adventures were not abolitionists, nor were they converted by the novel to the abolitionist approach. But they were antislavery, and now their image of slavery as an abstract evil was doubly confirmed by this moving personal narrative.

T HE truth is that Mrs. Stowe's volume did not so much make as harden opinion, an opinion that in 1852 already held fateful possibilities for the peace of 1850. The great Compromise had adjusted some specific issues. But no congressional enactment could erase what was in many men's minds—the moral challenge posed by the existence of slavery.

The capacity of the slavery issue to complicate all other questions was fully evident in the reactions to enforcement of the Fugitive Slave Act of 1850. This measure incorporated a complication of its own which was one of the oddest features of the sectional debate. The Southern doctrine of states' rights was not the simple, consistent thing it appeared to be on the surface. When it came to encouraging and extending slavery, the South could give aggressive support to federal power. To demand and secure a law that put all the resources of the federal authority behind the recovery of fugitive slaves, as the South had, was to urge the fullest sort of federal action.

Even South Carolina's Robert Barnwell Rhett, one of the fieriest of extremists, nevertheless told his section that in putting through the Fugitive Slave Act it had violated the philosophy it was supposed to represent. Rhett further warned that the law could not be enforced because it transgressed

John Hale, New Hampshire senator and Free-Soil presidential candidate in 1852, was responsible for ending the practice of flogging on U.S. ships. Sailors cheered Hale's bill in 1850 but were less enthusiastic about another reform he instituted in 1862; it did away with the Navy's daily ration of grog.

William Yancey, whose oratory inflamed the South, was raised in the Northeast but moved back to the South at 19. Yancey did not regret the time spent in the North because it had made him a better farmer. He was a Southerner in politics, he explained, but "a Yankee . . . around my cattle sheds."

another Southern principle, respect for the will of the community, and that even a strong minority in the Northern states could prevent its execution.

Rhett's prediction proved only too accurate. Popular resentment of the act was intense in the North, and in a number of cities organized mobs attempted to rescue, and in some cases did rescue, fugitives from federal marshals. The most spectacular episode occurred in Boston and concerned a runaway named Anthony Burns. When the news of his capture spread through the city, a mass meeting was called at Faneuil Hall. Wendell Phillips, the patrician orator of abolitionism, spoke and boldly demanded: "I want that man set free in the streets of Boston. . . . If that man leaves the city of Boston, Massachusetts is a conquered State." The crowd, led by respected citizens, poured out to storm the courthouse but was repelled by federal marshals and 22 companies of state troops. Burns was taken back to bondage through streets draped in black and hung with flags, many at half-mast. It was later estimated that it had cost as much as $100,000 to apprehend and return Burns.

Several Northern states passed laws to obstruct the national law, attempting to interpose state power between the fugitive and the federal enforcers, and the supreme court of Wisconsin went to the length of declaring the Fugitive Slave Act to be unconstitutional.

The effect of the abolitionist propaganda and the opposition to the Fugitive Slave Act on the South was to stir that section to both anger and apprehension. Below the Mason-Dixon Line *Uncle Tom's Cabin* was widely read and reviewed—and universally denounced. Characteristically, Southerners had first to convince themselves that it was proper to criticize a woman, which they easily did by asserting Mrs. Stowe had unsexed herself by writing such a book, and then they pulled no punches—she was that "wretch in petticoats." They were irritated at what they considered her inaccuracies, but what really disturbed them was the blanket condemnation of the South implicit in her book —i.e., its suggestion that slavery had corrupted the whole of Southern culture. If great numbers of the Northern people subscribed to this belief, Southerners wondered, could the South safely remain in a political association with them? Would not the North inevitably try to erase the corrupting agent?

Divisive forces were again stirring in American life. How quickly they would flare to the surface would depend in part on the quality of the political leadership in Washington, and most heavily on the man in the White House.

FRANKLIN PIERCE was not the man to dominate any situation, placid or critical. Only 49 years of age in 1853, he had had rather limited experience with politics and politicians. Boyishly handsome, he was charming in manner and appealing in person, but he was irresolute and indecisive. It has been said that he would come to one conclusion in the morning and change it in the afternoon. A story was told about him in his native New Hampshire. A traveler stopped at a village inn and asked the landlord what sort of man Pierce was. "Waal," was the reply, "up here, where everybody knows Frank Pierce and where Frank Pierce knows everybody, he's a pretty considerable fellow, I tell you. But come to spread him out over this whole country, I'm afraid that he'll be dreadful thin in some places."

He was not so inconsequential as the cruel barbs depicted him, but he was easily swayed by the stronger men about him, by the party leaders in Congress and by such members of his Cabinet as Secretary of State William L. Marcy of

One of the most celebrated escapes from slavery was made in 1849 by a Richmond black who became known as Henry "Box" Brown. He was nailed in a crate and shipped by a confederate to Philadelphia abolitionists. When the crate was opened, Brown—who had been inside it 25 hours—popped out and in the startled silence said calmly, "How do you do, gentlemen?"

New York, a moderate who regarded the antislavery agitation as mere mischievous nonsense, and Secretary of War Jefferson Davis, who represented the passionate intention of the South to maintain the institution of slavery.

Amiable and convivial, Pierce liked the company of Southerners and sympathized with their political views. He was a sincere and well-meaning man, but he lacked breadth and vision. Like so many of his contemporaries in both parties and sections, he was devoted to the Compromise and wanted to preserve it. At the same time, like the others, he could not forgo seizing upon opportunities for partisan advantage, pushing for projects that were sure to disturb the peace of the Compromise.

Pierce had announced in his inaugural address that the Administration would pursue a spirited and aggressive foreign policy unrestrained by "any timid forebodings of evil from expansion." "Indeed," he proclaimed, "it is not to be disguised that our attitude as a nation and our position on the globe render the acquisition of certain possessions not within our jurisdiction eminently important for our protection, if not in the future essential for the preservation of the rights of commerce and the peace of the world." Pierce's pretentious language masked but thinly one of the impelling forces in the national character, the urge to expansion that had carried American boundaries to the Pacific. In raising again the banner of Manifest Destiny, Pierce was only restating a basic Democratic and American tenet. But this was not the moment to suggest expansion. Many in the North inevitably concluded that Pierce's purpose was to acquire territory suitable for slavery, in the warmer Latin lands to the south and especially Cuba. He could have chosen no surer course to rekindle the coals of sectional distrust.

Pierce did envision possible benefits for the South in his proposed program, but his policy as executed was essentially in the national interest. The Administration tried to expand American influence on the Honduras-Nicaragua coast, upheld American fishing rights in Canadian waters and concluded a commercial treaty with Japan. Just as the last accomplishment reflected the importance Americans attached to their growing trade with Asia, so also did Secretary Marcy's attempt to take over Hawaii by a treaty of annexation, which failed only because the Senate refused to consider the pact (it contained a controversial provision granting the islands immediate statehood). These actual and near achievements in the tradition of American imperialism stirred some applause but not the outburst of national pride that might otherwise have found expression. The political atmosphere was so supercharged with the slavery question that Americans were distracted from other issues.

The Whigs of the North watched suspiciously for Pierce to make a move to acquire territory for slavery, and soon their worst fears were confirmed by the Administration's actions in Cuba. In previous years American interest in this island had been vigorously expressed, and representatives of both parties had agreed that in certain contingencies it might be necessary for national safety to annex Cuba. But now people thought about Cuba only in relation to slavery. Some Southerners talked about bringing the island in as a new slave state, and military adventurers operating out of Southern ports and called "filibusters" hatched plans to seize it or other areas in Central America.

Without doubt Pierce meant to secure Cuba if he could, and for reasons that would have served both the nation and the South. He sent as minister to

Harriet Beecher Stowe wrote many books after "Uncle Tom's Cabin," most of them with the same crusader's fervor. One was a sensational criticism of the private life of England's poet Lord Byron, and it caused as much of a fuss in Britain as "Uncle Tom" had in the South. Feeling ran so high that Charles Dickens wished that "Mrs. Stowe was in the pillory."

Spain the swarthy Pierre Soulé of Louisiana, vivaciously French in manner and speech, and deeply committed to bringing the island under American dominion as part of the Southern slave system. Soulé's instructions from Secretary Marcy were to offer to buy Cuba; if Spain would not sell, he was to "detach" it, presumably by inciting a revolution. Before Soulé could implement this unusual directive, he received a new one from Marcy. Now Soulé was to meet with the American ministers to England and France, James Buchanan and John Y. Mason, and together they were to determine a procedure to acquire Cuba. The three diplomats met and composed the undiplomatic document that when published in America came to be known as the Ostend Manifesto. It stated that the United States should propose to purchase Cuba; if Spain refused, the government should consider if possession of Cuba was essential to national security; if the answer was in the affirmative, the United States would be justified in "wresting" Cuba from Spain. In brutal brevity, if America wanted Cuba badly enough it had every right to resort to war.

The publication of the document stirred a storm of indignation in the North, evoked both by revulsion at this naked diplomacy and by a belief that it was part of a Southern plot to seize the island. The Administration hastened to deny any responsibility for the actions of the ministers, and what was clearly intended as a trial balloon quietly collapsed. But the episode put the South in a bad light. There were obviously some Southern leaders who would extend the boundaries of slavery by any means.

The caption of this 1850 English cartoon—"Master Jonathan tries to smoke a Cuba but it doesn't agree with him!"—was a gloating comment on vain American efforts to seize the Spanish-held island. Nobody was more annoyed by U.S. attacks than the Spaniards. Rather than see the island taken, one official said darkly he "would prefer seeing it sunk in the Ocean."

LESS than four years after the passage of the Compromise, and within a year after President Pierce had voiced his hope that it would never be broken, the great adjustment was on the thin edge of dissolution. Diverse factors had brought it there—the irrepressible debate over slavery, the unyielding principles of good men, the shortsighted actions of politicians. Yet it still stood as a symbol of sectional peace and as an affirmation of the desire for national survival. If it had turned out to be no more than a guarded truce, still it prevented open warfare, and there were few who would deliberately shatter it.

Then in 1854 an event occurred that snapped the pent-up tensions and returned the rule of crisis. Like so many episodes of the period, it was not consciously planned and executed, but was born in politics and developed in chance. Men set out to do something that they thought would bring them an advantage. They had no intention of provoking discord, but in following their goals they were led to do unforeseen things that inevitably did stir the worst kind of dissension. Ironically, the incident that plunged the country again into division had its origin in the existence of the huge Western territories whose resources were the surest guarantee of future national greatness.

The Western frontier pulsed with population movements throughout the '50s. Farmers began to push into the plains once thought too arid for cultivation. Even farther to the west, emigrants still pressed in substantial numbers to the Pacific coast and into the New Mexico and Utah Territories. Two new Western states, Minnesota and Oregon, came into the Union. During the last years of the decade, gold and silver were discovered in the Pikes Peak region and in the Sierra Nevada, and prospectors rushed in to lay the basis for the future Colorado and Nevada. It was evident that most of the area between the Mississippi and California would soon be settled. It was also evident that this region would have to be connected with the rest of the country by a faster form of transportation than the prevailing horse-and-wagon mode.

When Americans after 1840 thought about fast transportation over long distances, they thought, of course, of railroads. As the '50s opened, men in all sections were talking about a transcontinental railroad, a great line that would bind the nation with iron bands. The new tracks would begin at some point in the Mississippi Valley that had good connections with the East and would run from there to California. Private enterprise should construct the road, but as it was a truly national project the federal government should provide generous financial assistance. Everybody agreed on the need for such a road. But when it came to deciding the Mississippi Valley terminus, accord ended and sectional disagreement broke out.

Because of the expense involved, only one line could be built, and its route became a subject of contention between the sections. The discussion proceeded not on an engineering and technical basis—where was the best place to locate the line?—but on a political level: which section should receive the reward of the road? The two routes that commanded the most serious consideration were from Chicago and New Orleans. Both offered certain advantages, and both suffered from some handicaps. The Southern route provided a shorter passage to the coast and for part of its course ran through the already settled areas of Texas and New Mexico. But surveys indicated that it would have to pass through territory owned by Mexico. To remove this problem, Secretary of War Jefferson Davis, an enthusiastic proponent of the Southern road, persuaded President Pierce to negotiate with Mexico for the sale of this strip of land, and by the Gadsden Purchase of 1853 it became an American possession. The Northern route, in turn, had to overcome the objection that west of Iowa and Missouri it would lead through wilderness country.

Railroad considerations and others—the settlement of the West, the material expansion of the nation—were in the mind of Stephen A. Douglas when in January of 1854 he rose in the Senate to offer what would become the most fateful piece of legislation of the decade. The Little Giant had no impression that he was doing anything especially memorable, and he had no intention of provoking sectional division. As Chairman of the Committee on Territories, he introduced a simple bill to organize the Nebraska Territory in the region west of Iowa and Missouri.

In its original form, Douglas' bill contained nothing about the status of slavery in the territorial stage, but simply stated that when Nebraska became a state it could decide as it pleased about the institution. Presumably the territorial question was already covered by the Missouri Compromise of 1820—Nebraska was north of 36° 30', the dividing line between slavery and freedom in the old Louisiana Purchase region. But now Southern senators of his party, running for re-election and in need of an issue to impress their constituents, demanded that Douglas add a clause that would reopen the slave issue—in effect nullifying the Missouri Compromise in Nebraska.

WHAT followed was a tragic example of how political exigencies could influence the determination of a delicate issue and of how men could be led to do things they had not contemplated. The Southern senators who wanted to change the bill were from the border states, and they acted as much for motives of local popularity as for principle. But once the cry of Southern rights was raised the whole South had to support the alterations, if for no other

Commodore Matthew Perry, looking distinctly oriental in this Japanese portrait, was responsible for opening up the long-isolated empire of Japan for U.S. commerce. Appearing in the harbor of Yedo Bay with an impressive fleet, Perry overawed the Japanese with American arms and cajoled the emperor with gifts, including a toy train. He got rice and fish in return.

Former Democrat Lyman Trumbull, upset by his party's proslavery stand, broke away in 1856 and became a prominent Republican. He was a senator at the time—having won an Illinois election over a rival named Abraham Lincoln.

Former Whig Orville Browning could not make up his mind. He turned Republican, was a friend of Lincoln, opposed his presidential candidacy, edited his inaugural speech, later went against him again—and ended up a Democrat.

Former Free-Soiler George Julian was made a vice president of the Republican party at its first convention in 1856. A strong abolitionist, Julian was an ascetic man who neither smoked nor drank. His favorite food: bread and milk.

reason than that the North opposed them. And Douglas, to placate his Southern colleagues, had to consent to some changes. He added a provision conceding that the status of slavery in Nebraska was not settled but would have to be determined by popular sovereignty. But still the Southerners asked for more; one of them insisted that he would offer an amendment specifically repealing the Missouri Compromise if Douglas did not. Douglas once again yielded. "By God, sir, you are right," he is said to have replied, "and I will incorporate it in my bill, though I know it will raise a hell of a storm."

The final bill contained wording specifically repealing the Compromise and creating two territories, Nebraska and Kansas, in place of one. The apparent understanding was that perhaps Kansas, lying just west of slaveholding Missouri, might be won for the South.

Douglas, intent on pushing his bill to passage, had conceded too much. There was an outburst of fury in the North. Salmon P. Chase and five of his antislavery colleagues issued a statement denouncing the bill as "a gross violation of a sacred pledge; as a criminal betrayal of precious rights; as part and parcel of an atrocious plot." A popular newspaper poem depicted Douglas as a puppet of the South:

> The Dropsied Dwarf of Illinois
> By brother sneaks called, 'Little Giant,'
> He who has made so great a noise
> By being to the Slave Power pliant.

More alarming for Douglas' immediate purpose, he had stirred rebellion in his own party. Many Northern Democrats refused to support the measure.

Douglas had persuaded Pierce, who at first had tried to stay out of the controversy, to endorse the measure, thus giving it official status, and now the Administration threw its full weight for passage. Even with presidential pressure behind him, Douglas could not drive the bill through Congress until May. The vote on the Kansas-Nebraska Act was ominously sectional. Practically all the Southern members of Congress of both parties voted for it. Half of the Northern Democrats in the House voted against it; others wanted to but were held in line by the force of party discipline.

A STRANGELY purposeless episode was now closed. Douglas had passed a bill in a form he had not intended. The South had won a victory it should not have tried for and was not sure it wanted. If Douglas' motives were hazy, those of the Southern leaders were inexplicable. Some of them undoubtedly convinced themselves that it was possible for the South to win Kansas through popular sovereignty. The possibility was bare enough. The South, with its limited population, simply could not send enough people into a territory to compete successfully in an honest contest. Most Southern members of Congress knew this. Old Sam Houston voiced a typical reaction: "The South has not asked for it. . . . I, as the most extreme Southern Senator upon this floor, do not desire it. If it is a boon that is offered to propitiate the South, I, as a Southern man, repudiate it. I reject it. I will have none of it." Other Southerners who agreed with Houston still reasoned that if a victory was offered them they might as well take it.

Essentially Southerners acted as they did for emotional and abstract reasons. The Charleston *Mercury* put the Southern case perfectly: "There is no alternative for the South. When the North presents a sectional issue, and tenders battle upon it, she must meet it, or abide all the consequences of a victory easily won, by a remorseless and eager foe." For the satisfaction of upholding a principle, the South had let itself be placed in the position of seeming to attack sectional harmony.

The Kansas-Nebraska Act struck down the last vestiges of the truce of 1850. The measure intensified every sectional division in the country. The new law, declared Senator Charles S. Sumner of Massachusetts, was in one sense "the best Bill on which Congress ever acted," because it "makes all future compromises impossible.... Who can doubt the result?" It destroyed the faltering Whig party as a national political organization. Southern Whigs, angered beyond endurance at their Northern colleagues, drifted into the Democratic camp. Northern Whigs, dispirited as they saw their party disintegrating, lapsed into silence or inactivity. The act convinced many Northern Democrats that the South controlled their party and would exercise its power for purely Southern interests. It aroused the whole North to a fever pitch of anger.

The full weight of the popular fury fell on Douglas. He could travel to his home in Chicago, he said bitterly, by the light of his own burning effigies. He was compared to Benedict Arnold and Judas Iscariot, and some women in Ohio mockingly presented him with 30 pieces of silver.

This cartoon, drawn in 1860 when Stephen Douglas lost the presidential election, shows how much the Nebraska Act of 1854 cost him politically. Douglas was a prime subject for cartoonists. He was described in a Republican handbill as "about five feet nothing in height. . . . a red face, short legs, and a large belly. . . . talks a great deal, very loud, always about himself."

T HE Kansas-Nebraska Act killed the Whig party, but it brought into being a new one that voiced the aspirations of but one section, the majority North. The Republican party was born in the year the act was passed. In the tradition of American political parties, it appeared spontaneously, at first on the local level. All over the North, in cities, towns and villages, men gathered in meetings to denounce the Kansas-Nebraska Act and demand its repeal. Most of them were Whigs, but a fair number of Democrats were represented. Each meeting set up some kind of organization, and the members gave themselves a name. In most instances, they were "Anti-Nebraska" men, and sometimes "Republicans." The movement swelled and spread, and the professional politicians took notice of it and then, in one state after another, took it over. Suddenly it was a party—and, even before the end of 1854, a major party. In the elections of that year it sent a large delegation to Congress and won control of numerous Northern state governments.

At its inception the Republican party stood for only one principle—exclusion of slavery from every territory. To continue as a party, to take over the national government, it would have to add to its program; it would have to represent the desires of those Northern economic groups for which antislavery alone was not enough. That would come in the future. For the present it was enough that one of the major parties was frankly sectional. The other, the Democratic, was not as yet completely sectional, but increasingly people in the North believed it was. The lines were being drawn hard and fast.

All these things the Kansas-Nebraska Act had done, but they could not have been done if the Northern and Southern peoples had not been disposed to accept them. Douglas and the other politicians had only fanned a fire that had never been quenched. Crisis had threatened in 1850 and had been followed by conditional compromise and tremulous peace. Now crisis had returned. Henceforth it would reign without respite.

Discovering the pleasures of play

LEISURE as an end in itself was joyously discovered by 19th Century America, and the country went on a binge of pleasure-seeking which belied its puritanical past and confounded foreign observers. Until then the idea that the devil alone found work for idle hands was so well entrenched that Michel Chevalier, a visiting French economist, said that democracy was "too new a comer upon the earth to have been able as yet to organize its pleasures and amusements."

By the last half of the century, however, people filled amusement parks, theaters and variety halls, learned the latest dances, took part in newfangled sports like baseball, and organized elaborate outings. The need for recreation and culture first asserted itself in the big cities, where money was easier to earn and more freely spent than in the rural areas. Steady attendance helped usher in a golden age for American theater and brought wealth to showmen such as Phineas T. Barnum. But countryfolk soon sought amusement as well; gay circus wagons rolled through the hinterlands, and county fairs featured balloon ascensions, tightrope walkers and horse races. It was as if, said a surprised English visitor, "the people had no other occupation than sight-seeing."

SWIRLING DANCERS enliven a hop at West Point in this Winslow Homer engraving of 1859. Cadets now had to be as expert in the once-maligned waltz and polka as in riding and fencing.

DARING AERIALISTS exhibit their skills on a variety-hall poster (right). The act's name is a tribute to the fame of Blondin, a Frenchman who first crossed the falls on a high wire in 1859.

NIAGARA LEAP BY THE WONDERFUL BUISLAY FAMILY.

Outdoors, an array of sports for watchers and players

AMERICANS have always criticized their own state of physical fitness, and never more than in the middle 1800s. Ralph Waldo Emerson complained of the "invalid habits of this country," and Thomas Wentworth Higginson, a Massachusetts abolitionist, asked: "Who in this community really takes exercise?" Skating was Higginson's notion of exercise, and he helped make it so popular that one season 200,000 skaters jammed the ponds of New York City's Central Park. The Eastern colleges developed a variety of football that was so disorganized enthusiastic spectators were sometimes carried into the play. In the 1850s baseball had already come a long way from the days when first base was where third now is and runners could be put out by being hit with a thrown ball. By 1864 a prophetic writer could say: "This game . . . bids fair to become the national pastime."

TEAMS OF BOXERS square off in a version of the battle royal; uninjured boxers presumably substituted for their damaged teammates until only one side was still standing. Boxing was unlawful almost everywhere until the turn of the century; by then the rules called for gloves and a system of rounds.

Harvard freshmen and sophomores prepare for the kickoff in an 1857 interclass football game.

BASEBALL CLUBS called the Knickerbockers *(left)* and the Excelsiors *(right)* are separated by a top-hatted umpire in this 1858 photograph. By that time there were 25 organized clubs in the country. Mark Twain later called the game "the very outward and visible expression of the drive and push and rush and struggle of the raging, tearing, booming 19th Century."

Any number could play; the purpose was to push, throw or kick the ball over the opposing goal.

A TROTTING MATCH between a pair of famous stallions, Ethan Allen *(right)* and George M. Patchen, is depicted in a lithograph. No county fair was considered official without trotting races, and even staid Boston society enjoyed them. Drivers and horses were nationally renowned and inspired heavy betting.

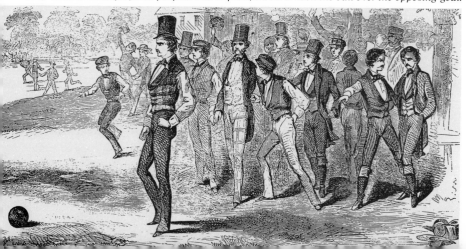

The "Original, Aboriginal, Erratic, Operatic" U.S. stage

THE mid-19th Century theater was a wild mixture. Shakespeare was a drawing card, but so was practically everything else. A house might play *Hamlet* one night, next the "Original, Aboriginal, Erratic, Operatic, Semi-Civilized and Demi-Savage Extravaganza of Pocahontas," and follow that with a melodrama in which the entire cast performed on horseback. Many perceptive critics winced at this mélange. In 1847 Walt Whitman, then on the *Brooklyn Eagle*, wrote, "where vulgarity (not only on the stage, but in front of it) is in the ascendant, and bad taste carries the day with hardly a pleasant point to mitigate its coarseness, the New York theatres . . . may be put . . . at the top of the heap."

Nevertheless, while audiences did throng to circus stunts and variety shows, they also cheered great actors like Edwin Forrest, the Booths and Fanny Kemble. In fact, they could get excited enough about their stars to stage major battles over them. In the famous Astor Place riot of 1849, adherents of Forrest stoned the theater where the English actor Charles Macready was playing, and before they could be dispersed by troops, 22 were dead and 36 injured. Like the rowdy audiences of the Elizabethan period, Americans inspired the best and worst in the theater and happily attended both.

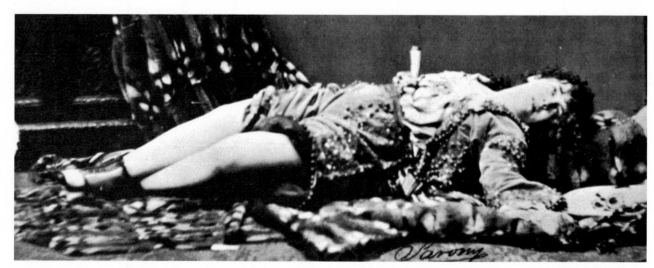

Adah Isaacs Menken lies dying in one of the melodramas she loved. Her fame was due less to her skill than to her flesh-colored tights.

Food and frolic for the family

For those Americans who lived far from the cities entertainment was usually homemade. Most farm families lived in a solitude that is almost inconceivable today; during the winter, weeks often passed without the sight of a new face. Small wonder that with warm weather eager plans were made for

family get-togethers, like the one shown here in J. P. Hardy's painting, *Pic Nick*. This affair, held in Camden, Maine, was the occasion for both feasting and fun. At the right a girl has swapped bonnets with a male cousin, while another young lady tickles the violinist with a twig. Music was an important part of such outings, but the quality varied. "There was good singers there," one state-of-Mainer reported of another picnic, " . . . but I chanced to drift alongside Mis' Peter Bowden o' Great Bay, an' I couldn't help thinkin' if she was as far out o' town as she was out o' tune, she wouldn't get back in a day!"

65

4. THE RUMBLE OF VIOLENCE

THE senator called his speech "The Crime Against Kansas." It was a carefully prepared document, filled with the historical and classical allusions that he delighted in, and he had, as was his custom, rehearsed the delivery of it while standing before a large mirror, practicing gestures and facial expressions. Like all his set addresses it was lengthy. Charles Sumner would require two days in May of 1856 to put in the record the truth of what was happening to Kansas. He knew that what he was going to say was true because antislavery people in Kansas had written him accounts of the crimes committed by the adherents of slavery. Now he would tell the Senate and the country about the greatest of the crimes—the conspiracy of the Pierce Administration and Stephen A. Douglas and the South to make Kansas a slave state.

It did not occur to Sumner that his information might be incomplete or incorrect. Like so many men on both sides of the sectional controversy, he saw things in simple terms of black and white. The scene he thought was so clear and sharp was actually one of immense complexity. After the passage of the Kansas-Nebraska Act, both territories were thrown open for settlement. Few people were interested as yet in distant Nebraska, but settlers poured into Kansas in large numbers. Most of them were the kind of people who appeared in all newly opened territories. The great majority were farmers who had heard that the soil in Kansas was good. Others came to try their hand at land speculation or to pick up government jobs or to be lawless in an area

ADVOCATE OF PEACE Franklin Pierce is depicted as President by G.P.A. Healy. Honest and orthodox, Pierce endeavored to satisfy all factions and ended up pleasing none.

Senate colleagues jokingly referred to David Atchison, Southern firebrand in Kansas, as "President for a day." There was a 24-hour Sunday lapse between the Polk and Taylor Administrations; Atchison, President pro tem of the Senate, was next in the line of succession. He said he spent the day sleeping.

A "peace convention" of pro- and antislavery factions in Fort Scott, Kansas, ends in a rowdy brawl. The controversy even affected the courts: one Free State group was so angered by a proslavery judge's decisions that it set up a "Squatters Court," swearing in witnesses with a medical book for lack of a Bible.

where law was not yet firmly established. They came into a wild and yet lovely land. The prairies stretched before them like a sea of grass, and they moved through acres of sunflowers that towered above a man's head. Soon the cabins of farmers lined the river valleys and dotted the plains that were burning hot in summer and icy cold in winter. Along the Missouri River and farther to the west, ramshackle, slatternly little towns of wood sprang up—wooden houses, wooden hotels, wooden stores and always a large collection of wooden saloons and gambling halls.

UP to a point the settlement of Kansas followed the normal pattern of expansion on any agricultural frontier. Up to a point—and then there was a serious divergence. Some people came for a single purpose of principle, to make Kansas free or a slave state. In the Northeast the abolitionist organizations, often working through so-called emigrant aid companies, supplied moral and financial assistance to men who wanted to further freedom on the plains. In the South, communities took up collections to send to Kansas spirited young blades who were eager to uphold Southern rights.

This was a stimulated and abnormal emigration, and there was yet another abnormal element in the situation. The proslavery politicians of Missouri had no desire to see a free state develop on their western border, and some of them confidently believed that Kansas could be won for slavery. Indeed, one, Senator David R. Atchison, a convivial, bellowing giant who had been among the Southerners pressing Douglas to modify his original territorial bill, envisioned a tier of future slave states from Kansas to California. To accomplish his initial objective Atchison saw nothing wrong in exhorting his Missouri followers to cross over and vote in the Kansas territorial elections; such a course was only a proper defense against the aggression of the emigrant aid companies. "When you reside within one day's journey of the territory," he told a Missouri audience, "and when your peace, your quiet and your property depend upon your action, you can, without an exertion, send five hundred of your young men who will vote in favor of your institutions." In his zeal to make Kansas a slave state, Atchison was prepared to do more than import voters. He confided in a letter to Jefferson Davis: "We will be compelled to shout, burn & hang, but the thing will soon be over."

Atchison's willingness to resort to force was matched by some of the free-state leaders in Kansas. One of them wrote to a New England capitalist who was backing emigration to the territory: "It looks very much like war, and I am ready for it, and so are our people. . . . Cannot your secret society send us 200 Sharps rifles as a loan till this question is settled? Also a couple of field-pieces?"

On both sides of the dispute, Kansas racial attitudes were very special, and Senator Sumner could never have understood them. Not all the settlers from the slave states, for example, wanted to establish slavery; at no time were there more than a couple of hundred blacks in the territory. The free-state people, on the other hand, were aggressively antislavery, but they were just as aggressively anti-Negro. They did not want slaves in Kansas, but neither did they want free blacks.

The election of the Kansas Territory's first legislature, held in 1855, was a farce. Over 6,000 votes were cast, many of them by Missourians, although there were probably not more than 1,500 legal voters in the entire territory.

A spurious vote of over 75 per cent was high even for a frontier election.

Not surprisingly, the proslavery forces won control of the legislature, and they proceeded to enact legislation legalizing slavery. The free-staters, convinced that the Pierce Administration would not permit a fair expression of opinion, now went to the length of acting extralegally. Without prior congressional approval, they elected delegates to a convention of their own which adopted a constitution excluding slavery. They then applied for admission, in effect laying their case before the country. President Pierce denounced their action as "revolutionary"; the government, he said, would use its full force to sustain the legal authorities of the territory.

There had always been some violence in Kansas, as there was in every frontier area. Men fought over land claims just because it was good Western form to fight. But now suddenly a new kind of violence, one with ideological overtones, broke on the scene. It was a frontier precursor of civil war. A proslavery settler killed an antislavery settler in a dispute about land boundaries. Angry talks and wild threats from the friends of both men sparked sudden action. An armed force of proslavery men marched on the free-state town of Lawrence, and only the intervention of the territorial governor averted a pitched battle.

On May 21, a federal marshal led a posse of 800 men, many of them Missourians, into Lawrence to arrest the free-state leaders. Although the marshal was acting under the mandate of a federal judge, the expedition had all the marks of a trumped-up affair. Senator Atchison accompanied it, as did several other men who had personal or political grudges against people in Lawrence, and at least one artillery piece traveled with the small army. The posse degenerated into a mob. The presses of two antislavery papers were thrown into the Kaw River, a hotel was burned and many private homes were looted. Before the avengers departed, one of their members, a sheriff, is said to have boasted: "Gentlemen, this is the happiest day of my life. I determined to make the fanatics bow before me in the dust and kiss the territorial laws. I have done it, by God."

Three days later there was grim reprisal. Among the men who had come to Kansas to battle for freedom was one called John Brown. Rugged, awesome, with eyes that seemed to burn into the future, "Old Brown," as he was usually called, knew he was God's instrument to destroy slavery. It had been revealed to him. Now he had a special mission to perform. Collecting six men who would follow him anywhere, he traveled to the town of Pottawatomie and supervised the killing of five proslavery settlers—he estimated five antislavery men had been murdered—watching without a quiver as the sinners were hacked to death with sabers.

Even if Charles Sumner had been apprised of the full intricacy of Kansas affairs, he would not have believed it. He did not deal with qualifications, but with morals and principles and stern justice. A large, handsome man with flowing ringlets, he was sincere, doctrinaire and humorless. He once said that he had got beyond thinking of individuals, which caused an acquaintance to snort that not even God Almighty had gone that far yet. Elected to the Senate in 1850 without a clear party affiliation, he had become a Republican in 1854 because that party promised to be the instrument that would destroy slavery, and the destruction of slavery was Sumner's great passion.

Robert Walker, "a mere whiffet of a man" of under 100 pounds, was one of 11 men who governed Kansas in seven years. A Democrat who freed his own slaves, he was dubbed "Isothermal" for his idea that slavery was dependent on climate—likely to fail in the chilly North, succeed in the warm South.

Colonel Edwin Sumner rallies U.S. troops before the hall where Free State Kansas legislators were holding a rump meeting. Sumner, who was ordered to disperse illegal organizations, attempted to break up the session. Free Staters said he was secessionist, but he became a Union general in the Civil War.

He was confident and righteous that May day when he flung back his scholar's head and began to roll out his oration on Kansas. The Senate galleries, which had filled in anticipation of the event, must have been at first somewhat disappointed. They heard only the familiar Republican account of what was happening in Kansas. But then the speaker aroused his audience by employing an attention-catching metaphor—the crime against Kansas was "the rape of a virgin territory, compelling it to the hateful embrace of slavery" —and he shocked his senatorial colleagues by launching into personal invective rare even for that hard-bitten age. He struck hardest at South Carolina's Andrew P. Butler, who was absent: "The Senator from South Carolina has read many books of chivalry, and believes himself a chivalrous knight, with sentiments of honor and courage. Of course he has chosen a mistress to whom he has made his vows and who, although ugly to others, is always lovely to him; although polluted in the sight of the world, is chaste in his sight—I mean the harlot, Slavery."

OFFICIAL Washington seethed with excitement after Sumner ended his philippic. The Southerners were enraged. One of them, Preston Brooks, a member of the House and a young kinsman of Senator Butler, resolved to take direct action. By his Southern code Sumner had to be punished, and Brooks methodically considered what penalty to mete out. He decided against challenging Sumner to a duel; the New Englander would not accept, and anyway one did not call out a social inferior. The offense called for chastisement, and Brooks deliberated whether he should use a horsewhip or a walking stick for the punishment.

Reflecting that Sumner was a larger man and might wrest the whip from him, thus forcing him to take the senator's life, he decided on a stick. Selecting a gutta-percha cane, he went to the Senate when it was not in session. Sumner was seated at his desk writing. Brooks held back for a while: a female visitor was in the chamber, and a Southern gentleman could not commit violence in the presence of a lady. Finally the woman left, and Brooks walked up to Sumner. He announced that he had come to punish a slanderer and then struck—the accounts differ—a light warning tap or a heavy blow on Sumner's head. He continued to strike, forgetting as frenzy gripped him that he had meant only to chastise. Sumner, confused under the rain of blows, rose straight up from his chair, his agonized effort wrenching the bolted desk from the floor. Brooks continued to beat his now helpless quarry until the cane broke, and then he struck with the butt.

Several Southern senators, attracted by the commotion, came up, as did Douglas, and stood watching. But none made a move to interfere, and there were even some cries of approval. Finally two members of the House rushed in to restrain Brooks, other men intervened and the semiconscious Sumner was taken away.

The reactions to the episode were strikingly different in the North and the South. Northerners viewed the attack as an atrocity, as an example of typical Southern ruffianism. "Bully" Brooks had done to Sumner what the bully boys of slavery had done to the town of Lawrence. Such primitive actions were to be expected from products of the slave system, Ralph Waldo Emerson explained, because in the South man himself was no more than an animal. But in the South applause for Brooks was almost universal. He was a courtly gen-

Entitled "Southern Chivalry," a Northern view of the beating of Senator Charles Sumner by Preston Brooks shows Southerners enjoying the sight, and even holding back Sumner's friends. Years before, Sumner's father, speaking more prophetically than he knew, remarked of the slave issue: "Our children's heads will some day be broken . . . on this question."

tleman who had defended the honor of his family and his state. "Far from blaming Brooks," said a Richmond newspaper, "we are disposed to regard him as a conservative gentleman, seeking to restore to the Senate that dignity and respectability of which Abolition Senators are fast stripping it." From all over the section he received presents of canes and offers of more if he needed them in his work. Students at the University of Virginia offered to send him one with a heavy gold top which would have on it the device of "the human head, badly cracked and broken." Resigning his seat to permit his district to voice its opinion, Brooks was re-elected almost unanimously.

It was three years before Sumner, now a genuine martyr, recovered sufficiently to resume his Senate seat on a regular basis. Many hostile newspapers charged that he was shamming and afraid to return—"This most ridiculous of humbugs fairly stinks in the nostrils of the American people," ran one editorial comment—but Massachusetts elected him to another full term.

The Brooks-Sumner affair revealed more than a sectional divergence regarding standards of conduct. Americans increasingly were turning to violence as a way of settling their differences over slavery. After 1856 many members of Congress came to the sessions armed. Knives and pistols were flourished in debate. Collisions occurred between Northern and Southern members. The House once witnessed two dozen Representatives swinging fists and rolling on the floor. Possible bloodshed was averted when somebody grabbed a Southern congressman's hair and pulled off an unsuspected wig; astonishment was so great that anger dissolved in laughter.

Southerners, still cherishing the code of rural gentry society, regularly flung challenges to duel at Northern members, who, ignorant of the practice, loftily declined. But one Northern Senator, Ohio's "Bluff Ben" Wade, discovered a safe way to accept—choose a weapon the chivalry was unfamiliar with. Challenged, he selected squirrel rifles at 20 paces and met a hasty withdrawal. The violence in congressional halls was an ominous portent. Americans everywhere were getting beyond the stage where they were satisfied merely to argue about slavery.

HARDLY had the excitement over the caning of Sumner abated when the country entered on the campaign of 1856. The Democrats, the old, staid and conservative party, endorsed the Kansas-Nebraska Act and popular sovereignty, and nominated an old, staid and conservative candidate, James Buchanan of Pennsylvania. The Republicans, young, aggressive and confident, nominated John C. Frémont, famous for his explorations of the Western wilderness. Still a one-idea party, they denounced Kansas-Nebraska and slavery expansion, though they added planks approving internal improvements and a privately constructed transcontinental railroad.

Also in the contest was another one-idea organization, the American party. Originating in the resentment against the great flood of immigrants, it was antiforeign and anti-Catholic. It had come into being as a secret society, complete with passwords and grips. When members were asked what the society stood for they were instructed to reply: "I know nothing." As a result they were dubbed "Know-Nothings." The party recruited a strong following from native Americans who sincerely believed that the alien influx represented a danger to American institutions and from Whigs on the way out of their party who balked at joining the Republicans. In the elections of 1854 the Americans

These campaign pictures of Buchanan (below) and Frémont and his wife (above) were used by Frémont partisans in 1856. They credit him with securing California and deride his opponent for signing the Ostend Manifesto, which urged U.S. seizure of Cuba. In sponsoring the manifesto, Buchanan broke his own rule: "Be quiet and discreet and say nothing."

scored some spectacular successes, but soon they began to break apart on the inevitable slavery issue, dividing into Northern and Southern Americans. In 1856, however, the divided party joined ranks to nominate former President Millard Fillmore.

The campaign was marked by wild enthusiasm. Confidently taking the offensive, the Republicans chanted their slogan in parades and at mass meetings: "Free Soil, Free Speech, and Frémont," and they employed "Bleeding Kansas" and "Bleeding Sumner" as effective symbols of slavery's tyranny. They aroused wide support in the North but not enough to win. Yet they came close. The November election disclosed that Buchanan had 174 electoral votes to Frémont's 114 and that the Democrats had a majority of both houses of Congress. Eleven Northern states had gone to Frémont; if the votes in two others had shifted in his favor he would have been President. All in all, the results were such as to make the South apprehensive for the future. It now seemed quite possible that a sectional Northern party could secure control of the government.

Into the White House in March 1857 came James Buchanan, "Old Buck." His professional background was impressive—10 years in the House and almost 11 in the Senate, Secretary of State and minister to Russia and England. Because his adult life had been spent in a succession of offices, intimates referred to him as "Old Public Functionary" or "Old Pub Func." Impressive too was his person, a tall, heavy figure crowned by a kindly, ruddy face and a mane of white hair. An appealing air of romance clung to him. The sweetheart of his youth had died after a misunderstanding between them, and the contrite Buchanan had never married. He liked the society of women and always he reminded them of his blighted love.

The impressiveness ended with the outer man. Buchanan was sincere and well-meaning, but like Pierce he was indecisive. It was said that he was dominated by the Southerners in his party. The accusation does not entirely explain Buchanan. He was not consciously proslavery, but he viewed the issue in a narrow, legalistic perspective—whatever was lawful was right and was to be protected. "The Bible for Heaven," he liked to say, "the Constitution for earth." Physically infirm and easily perturbed, Buchanan longed above all else for personal and political repose.

In a Know-Nothing cartoon, Irish and German immigrants, represented by whiskey and beer, make off with the ballots, while other foreigners beat up voters. But in Baltimore the Know-Nothings themselves gave thugs weapons to "plug" unfriendly voters; the thugs became known as "plug-uglies."

HE would get little of either in his Administration. In the very year that he took office a financial panic struck the country, followed by a severe depression. Essentially the economic trouble was an outgrowth of the vast expansion of productive facilities in the '50s. Production had outrun demands; inevitably the boom had to end in a crash. The resulting depression was as bad as any the country had yet suffered. Banks halted specie payments and then collapsed, stock prices fell, business firms suspended operations and unemployed workers roamed the Northern cities shouting "Bread or blood."

The depression was national in its scope, but instead of uniting the sections in a common experience it had the effect of intensifying sectional division. Although the South felt some of the impact, it was not so hard hit as the North; it had as yet engaged in practically no industrial expansion, and its principal product, cotton, still commanded good prices. Southerners were confirmed in their conviction that their system was superior, and many concluded that the agricultural section would have a brighter future outside the Union. "The wealth of the South is permanent and real," exclaimed *De Bow's Review*, the voice of Southern economic thought, "that of the North fugitive and fictitious."

The Northern classes most affected, manufacturers and farmers, drew from the depression a different lesson: the dislocation had been caused by the policies of a Southern-controlled Democratic Administration, and this same combination was holding back future national growth. Material forces were impelling the principal Northern power groups toward an alliance with the antislavery impulse and the Republican party.

In his inaugural address Buchanan had dropped an intriguing piece of information. The Supreme Court, he said, would shortly hand down a decision on the question of slavery in the territories that should end all agitation. His revelation was indiscreet. For a President to have prior knowledge of a Court decree was highly unusual, and there were charges that somebody on the bench had tipped him off. The truth was even stranger: Buchanan had actually played a part in deciding the nature of the decision.

Even while Dred Scott was suing for his freedom, the sheriff guarding him hired him out at five dollars a month. Though the Supreme Court ruled against him, Scott was freed by his owner. He worked for a good many years as a porter at a hotel in St. Louis, where he died peacefully at the age of 58.

The case he referred to was *Dred Scott vs. Sanford,* and the Court announced its finding two days after the inauguration. In origin and history the Dred Scott case was bewilderingly complicated. Scott was a Missouri slave who at one time had been the property of an army surgeon. His owner had taken him into free areas where slavery was forbidden by the Missouri Compromise, and finally had returned to Missouri. At this point the complexities began. The surgeon died, and Scott, at the instigation of a local lawyer, brought a suit for his freedom on the ground that his sojourn in free territory had made him free. A state circuit court held in his favor, but the decision was reversed by the state supreme court. Then the surgeon's widow remarried. Under Missouri law, ownership of Scott was thereupon transferred to her brother, John Sanford, a New York resident who was executor of the surgeon's will. Scott's change of residence made it possible for his lawyer to get the case into the federal courts. It was a test case under Republican and antislavery auspices, but, as was evident when it made its way up to the Supreme Court, the South was eager to meet the test.

The Court that sat on the case was composed of nine justices. Seven were Democrats, five of them from the South, and two were Republicans. Presiding as Chief Justice was the cadaverous old Roger B. Taney, who had been appointed by Andrew Jackson. It was a prickly case, and the justices approached it with reluctance. Involved were two principal points. Was Scott entitled to bring a suit? And was he free as a result of the prohibition of slavery in the Missouri Compromise? At first Taney and the Democratic majority inclined to avoid the broader considerations and dismiss the case for want of jurisdiction. Then the two Republican members let it be known that they would prepare opinions discussing the whole question of the power of Congress to regulate slavery in the territories. Taney and his colleagues decided at that point that perhaps they should consider the case in its larger aspects. One of the justices communicated this information to Buchanan, who replied that he was glad the Court was going to meet the challenge. At the same justice's suggestion, the President put some pressure on one of the Northern Democratic members to join in the decision of the majority.

In the 7 to 2 decision, there were actually several opinions: each of the nine members wrote a separate one. But Taney's opinion embodied the essence of

Though a Northern journal declared that Chief Justice Roger Taney would "be held in infamous remembrance" for his refusal to free the slave Dred Scott, Taney personally hated slavery and liberated his own slaves. A Catholic, he would often wait in line with Negroes at the confessional door.

the majority reasoning and was regarded as the official decision. The Chief Justice laid down two judicial principles. One, Scott could not bring a suit in the federal courts because he was not a national citizen. No black who was a descendant of slaves, and by inference no black of any origin, could ever become a national citizen. Two, Scott was not free even though he had lived in federal territory closed to slavery. The Missouri Compromise prohibition was unconstitutional. Slaves were property, specifically recognized as such in the Constitution; and by the Fifth Amendment, Congress could pass no law depriving persons of property. Any Congressional exclusion of slavery in any territory was illegal. Indeed, Congress had an obligation to extend its protection over slave property in the territories.

The furor was wide and loud. Southerners hailed the decision as a judicial endorsement of the Southern position on the territorial question and announced that they expected the North to accept it. But Republicans denounced it and warned that if they secured control of the government they would change the composition of the Court and have the decision overruled. One Republican newspaper snorted that the decision had no more moral weight than the opinion of any group meeting in a Washington barroom.

There was, to be sure, some doubtful law in the decision and some extremely bad politics. The Court had intervened in a political controversy and clearly on one side. It had held the platform of a major party to be unlawful. More, it had implied, although probably not intentionally, that slavery could go anywhere, even into free states. If Republicans were aghast at the decision, Northern Democrats were only slightly less shocked. For if Congress could not bar slavery from a territory, neither could a territorial legislature, and popular sovereignty was a mockery.

POPULAR sovereignty was at the moment getting a rough baptism in still-bleeding Kansas. Buchanan appointed as governor wizened little Robert J. Walker, a politician of some distinction, with instructions to get a statehood movement under way. Walker understood that he was to run a fair election and that the President would back him up. But Buchanan had certain reservations. Both he and Walker were interested in bringing Kansas in as a Democratic rather than as a slave state. But above all "Old Buck" wanted to bring Kansas in—admission would eliminate a sore situation that was making votes for the Republicans. He did not care if Kansas entered as a slave state if the procedure was, on the surface, properly legal. Neither the President nor his governor understood the bitter conflicting currents in the territory.

But Walker received a shocking insight when he arrived in the raw territory. In his inaugural address he declared that the constitution for the proposed state would have to be submitted to a popular vote. He added that climate made it unlikely that slavery could flourish in Kansas. At a banquet the next evening he repeated the statements. His proslavery audience listened in anger, and one burly man rose up and contemptuously told Walker that he was a "pigmy" and would be driven out of the territory if he failed to toe the line.

At the time of Walker's arrival in Kansas, a campaign was under way to elect a state constitutional convention, called by the proslavery legislature. The governor urged the free-staters to participate, but they abstained, some because they did not trust a Buchanan appointee, others because they were

Henry du Pont, the largest supplier of explosives to the Union during the Civil War, inherited his father's business when he was only 38 and served as manager until 1889, when he was 77. At the Du Pont works in Wilmington, Delaware (below), he was a paternalistic employer; his men called him "the General," and it is said he knew each of them by name.

unable to get themselves registered, still others because they did not want to be registered as voters and hence as taxpayers. With little opposition, the proslavery forces won firm control of the convention. The convention held its sessions in Lecompton through the autumn of 1857. While it was deliberating, the regular election for a new legislature fell due.

This time the free-state people, now believing in Walker, did vote. The usual influx of Missouri voters did not occur. Deterred by Walker's threat to call in the army and knowing that the free-staters would meet an invasion with force, Atchison's bands stayed at home. The proslavery Democrats resorted to stuffing the ballot boxes. One precinct with six houses reported 1,628 votes, nearly all Democratic. But the governor had promised to throw out all fraudulent returns, and he kept his word. As a result, the free-staters won clear control of the legislature.

A month later the Lecompton convention approved a constitution establishing slavery in the territory. But since it was now clear that such a document was unlikely to receive popular approval, the leaders decided against submitting the whole constitution for ratification. Instead, the voters were asked to choose a constitution either "with" or "without" slavery. If the latter provision carried, no more slaves could be brought in, but existing titles in slave property would continue, so that either way Kansas would be (if only technically) a slave state. Such an option was a farce if not a fraud.

Nevertheless Buchanan persuaded himself that the Lecompton convention represented the true sentiment of Kansas. He let it be known that he would recommend to Congress that the Kansans vote on the meaningless choice presented to them. His position stirred Walker into an angry resignation.

Even more infuriated was Douglas, who knew that his state and section were aflame with anger at the Lecompton trick. "By God, sir," the Democratic leader exploded to a newspaper editor, "I made Mr. James Buchanan, and by God, sir, I will unmake him." He rushed to see the President. It was an angry interview. Buchanan, with the obstinacy of a weak man, clung to his decision. In his fussy manner the President reminded Douglas that no Democrat had successfully defied a President of his party since Andrew Jackson's time. The Illinois senator shot back: "Mr. President, I wish you to remember that General Jackson is dead."

In Kansas the outraged free-staters refused to participate in the referendum. On December 21 the Lecompton Constitution was approved by a vote of over 6,000 for "with" slavery as against fewer than 600 for "without."

BUT the free-staters still had a card to play. The new legislature had met in special session early in December and decided to submit the *whole* Lecompton Constitution to another referendum on January 4. In this second contest the proslavery people refrained from voting, and the document was snowed under by 10,000 votes. No election in Kansas really reflected the popular will accurately, and this one scarcely more than the others. Still, the picture was clear enough and should have been visible to Buchanan: A majority of the Kansas people opposed slavery.

Buchanan misread the situation completely. He still accepted the first referendum as binding. The second election made no impression at all on him. He sent the Lecompton Constitution to Congress and demanded that the Democrats support it as a party measure.

Cyrus McCormick (above), inventor of the reaper, also made the less expensive dropper (below). Although such machinery enabled the North to raise bumper crops even during the war, skeptics called the reaper "an extravagant Yankee contrivance," and the London "Times" described it as "a cross between a flying machine, a wheelbarrow and an Astley chariot."

Thoroughly aroused, Douglas opposed the Lecompton bill when it came up for consideration and rallied enough Western Democratic votes to insure the measure's defeat. The bill never came to a final vote in its original form. Instead Congress passed a measure calling for still another Kansas vote on the entire Lecompton Constitution. Once again it was decisively rejected by the Kansans. Southern Democrats who had fought for Lecompton now looked at the "Little Giant" with questioning and hostile eyes.

Douglas came up for re-election in 1858, and he faced the political fight of his life. The Administration not only failed to offer him support; it openly worked against him. But Douglas was worried less by his own party's attacks from Washington than by the nature of his opposition in Illinois. He had to run against the most formidable candidate the Republicans could offer, Abraham Lincoln.

Douglas knew his rival well, knew him as an adroit politician, as a resourceful campaigner and above all as a dangerously effective stump speaker. Lincoln was an almost unknown figure nationally. A dozen years earlier he had served an undistinguished two-year term in the House and then had disappeared from the national scene. But he had continued active in state politics. He had been the leading Whig in Illinois and now he was the leading Republican, with a reputation for political sagacity that was spreading throughout the Northwest. Nevertheless, it was only because Douglas was a national politician that the Illinois senatorial contest attracted wide attention. Lincoln, to gain prestige and to put Douglas on the defensive, challenged the senator to a series of debates, and Douglas, with some reluctance, accepted.

Long before the Lincoln-Douglas debates the two reportedly competed in another race, for the hand of Mary Todd. Instead of Stephen A. Douglas (above) she wed "Him who has the best prospect of being President," but Douglas was not a bitter man. Years later, young Robert Lincoln arrived at Harvard carrying a letter of introduction from Douglas.

THE ensuing discussions, reported at length in the press all over the country, immediately became famous as the Lincoln-Douglas debates. They brought into a new, sharp focus the fundamental issue before the American people. Both men were opposed to slavery and both wanted to keep it out of the territories. Douglas' opposition was passive. He believed that slavery was a decaying institution that would eventually disappear, and he saw no reason to irritate people by calling it wrong. But Lincoln thought that slavery was vital and dynamic, intent on expansion. He did not propose to abolish it in the states where it existed, but by congressional exclusion he wanted to bar it from the territories and place it, in his phrase, in a state of "ultimate extinction." Above all, Lincoln insisted that the problem of slavery could never be dealt with unless the moral aspect was recognized. "That is the real issue," the candidate said. "That is the issue that will continue in this country when these poor tongues of Judge Douglas and myself shall be silent. It is the eternal struggle between these two principles—right or wrong—throughout the world."

The two men debated the issue all across Illinois. At each meeting thousands came to hear them, many traveling long miles over rutted prairie roads, and in dusty courthouse squares the crowds stood patiently for hours in the summer heat to hear the arguments. The physical contrast between the contestants was startling. Douglas, short, massive and aggressive, roared out his sentences like a confident lion. Lincoln, angular and awkward and towering to four inches over six feet, had a high and rather piping voice. But his logic gripped the thoughts of men.

Over and over in the debates Lincoln hammered away at the wrongness of slavery. He seemed to be thinking as much of the future as of the present election. At Freeport he asked Douglas a loaded question. Could the people of a territory exclude slavery prior to statehood? In reality he was asking: Was popular sovereignty still legal and practical despite the Dred Scott decision? The Little Giant, cornered, did his best. Yes, he said, the people of a territory could still exclude slavery, Supreme Court or no; they could accomplish the purpose by neglecting to adopt local laws for its protection.

Douglas had said the same thing before. But this was different. He had stated in a national forum that popular sovereignty was really an antislavery formula. Southern Democrats denounced in unmeasured terms what they called the Freeport Heresy. Douglas narrowly won re-election to the Senate, but he was no longer the unquestioned leader of his party or the idol of the North. A new and towering figure, who would loom ever larger, had been projected onto the political scene.

ANOTHER figure was about to make his last appearance. It would be dramatic, and it would rivet the attention of the whole country. Old John Brown had disappeared after his spectacular career in Kansas. He reappeared in the Northeast, and now he had a really grand plan to do God's work. He confided the outlines but not the details of it to six abolitionist leaders. These men entered eagerly into the conspiracy, even to the point of assuming code names, and were known as the "Secret Six." Their principal service was to provide Brown with financial assistance. He intended to seize a strong point in the mountain area of Virginia, set it up as a fortified base and operate from there to free slaves. Eventually he meant to take his charges into the hills, organize them into a kind of black state within the South and force a general emancipation.

It was a mad scheme—there was a record of insanity in Brown's family—but he had the iron will to execute it. As his first objective he fixed on Harpers Ferry, on the Potomac just across from Maryland. A federal arsenal was located there and he would need guns to arm the slaves. The old man had planned his moves like a general about to engage in battle. In July 1859 he rented a farm in Maryland about four miles north of Harpers Ferry. Gradually his followers drifted in. There were 21 of them in all, including five blacks and three of Brown's sons. Then the arms began to arrive in crates—200 rifles, 200 revolvers and 1,000 pikes specially manufactured for the slaves who would rise to greet him.

On the night of October 16, in raw, drizzly weather, Brown and 18 of his followers left the farmhouse. Brown drove off in a wagon and his men marched behind him, carrying their rifles under gray woolen shawls. They came to the covered railroad bridge over the Potomac and seized the lone watchman on duty. Leaving two men to guard the bridge, the raiders moved into Harpers Ferry. Most of the 3,000 inhabitants were sleeping, unaware that in a few hours their town would hold the horrified attention of the nation.

The economy of Harpers Ferry rested on its ordnance manufacture, which was carried on in a complex of government buildings—an armory, an arsenal, an enginehouse. Brown seized all of them, stationing himself and most of his men in the enginehouse. But now the man who had planned his campaign like a general was not thinking very clearly. He was splitting up his small force, and he was protecting his escape route over the river with only two

Abraham Lincoln, in this photograph taken before he was elected President, retains some aspects of the ungainly young circuit lawyer of earlier years. In those days, as he traveled from town to town, Lincoln was in the habit of sleeping in a homemade yellow flannel undershirt. Thus attired, he was described by a fellow lawyer as "the ungodliest figure I ever saw."

men. In fact, from the moment he entered the town he seemed to suffer a paralysis of decision—almost as if he actually was hoping for destruction.

He sent out some men to bring in the area's most prominent citizen, Colonel Lewis W. Washington, great-grandnephew of the first President. He instructed them to bring too a possession he had heard the colonel owned, a sword presented to George Washington by Frederick the Great. His men returned with Colonel Washington and the sword and a number of slaves. Eventually other captives were brought in, perhaps as many as 50. Brown buckled the sword around his waist and waited.

Soon the presence of the raiders became known in the town. Another watchman went to check on the railroad bridge and ran into bullets from Brown's guards. He escaped and gave the alarm. At the same time the night express of the Baltimore & Ohio was heard approaching, and a man went out to warn it that something was wrong at the bridge. A station baggageman walked toward the bridge and was shot down; he died 12 hours later in agony. He was the first victim of the liberators, and it was a bitter irony that he was a free black and a respected resident of Harpers Ferry. One citizen rode to the nearby county seat of Charles Town to ask for help. From there a call went out for the militia companies of the area to proceed to Harpers Ferry, and eventually 200 citizen soldiers collected in the town.

More aid was en route. Brown had permitted the eastbound train to continue on its way; at Monocacy the conductor telegraphed the news to his superiors, who passed it on to official Washington. President Buchanan acted with a decisiveness he did not display in other crises. A detachment of marines was ordered to Harpers Ferry. They went under the command of an army officer then in Washington on leave, Colonel Robert E. Lee. Accompanying them was a young cavalry lieutenant who also happened to be in Washington and who asked to go along, James Ewell Brown ("Jeb") Stuart.

Meanwhile, at Harpers Ferry the militia and armed townsmen had surrounded Brown and his men in their separate strongholds. Twice under white flags the old man tried to parley, but one of his men was captured and two were shot down. He lost other men, some picked off by lucky shots and some because they tried to break out—10 in all, finally, including two of his sons. The next day Colonel Lee's marines, who had arrived shortly before midnight, broke in the enginehouse doors and easily overpowered the defenders.

JOHN BROWN'S raid was finished. But John Brown in failure would now exert an effect that perhaps only he had foreseen. The federal government turned him and his surviving followers over to Virginia to be tried for treason against the state. The old man sat in his cell and issued a stream of letters and communications that found their way into print. In them he depicted himself as a man of God and a man of peace who wanted only to help the oppressed. For all his fanaticism he had a shrewd sense of propaganda, and now he was creating a new image of himself.

He fixed the image perfectly in his last speech at his trial. He had not come to Virginia to commit violence or revolution, he said, ignoring the fact of the rifles and the pikes. He had meant, he went on, only to liberate slaves without bloodshed as he had done in the West, which was a downright falsehood. But the Biblical majesty of his words deceived people everywhere and awed even his Southern audiences: "I say, I am yet too young to understand that

New Yorkers seeking to withdraw their deposits storm a Wall Street bank during the Panic of 1857. As a result of this depression large numbers of people were thrown out of work, and local government officials resorted to a variety of expedients to help them—including one of the first "make-work" projects, a large construction program in New York's new Central Park.

God is any respecter of persons. I believe that to have interfered as I have done . . . in behalf of His despised poor, was not wrong, but right. Now, if it is deemed necessary that I should forfeit my life for the furtherance of the ends of justice, and mingle my blood further with the blood of my children, and with the blood of millions in this slave country whose rights are disregarded by wicked, cruel, and unjust enactments—I submit: so let it be done!"

Brown moved the whole court, but rhetoric could not save him now. He was sentenced to death by hanging, and on a bright, crisp day in early December he was led from his cell to mount the scaffold. The Virginia government, fearing that an attempt might be made to rescue Brown, had ringed the village of Charles Town and the scene of the execution with militia. Up from Lexington came a detachment of Virginia Military Institute cadets under the command of an odd-looking professor named Thomas J. Jackson, one day to be known as "Stonewall." A white-haired old man attached himself to the ranks of cadets. He was Edmund Ruffin, a fierce zealot for Southern rights. A year and a half later as a volunteer aide at Fort Sumter he would fire one of the first shots of the Civil War. In the rear ranks of the Richmond Grays was a dark, dramatic young man who was making something of a name for himself on the stage. He could not know that at this scaffold a train of events was being set in motion that would one day cast him as the central actor in a great tragedy. His name was John Wilkes Booth.

The sheriff cut the rope and the trap came down. The figure of John Brown jerked in the air, and a legend was born and went marching into history.

John Brown was clean-shaven until authorities began to seek him for his part in the killing of several men in Kansas. Then he grew his familiar beard as a disguise—and adopted the alias Shubel Morgan. Brown spent much of his life on the run. To avoid creditors, he was forced to move repeatedly with his large family (he had seven children by his first wife, 13 by his second).

IN the North prominent Republicans hastened to condemn Brown's deeds and to disavow responsibility for them. But in the South their protestations were not believed. The Brown raid sent a chill of horror through the entire region. This was, said Southerners, an attempted slave insurrection incited from the outside. Brown had not acted alone. If the Republican or the Northern leaders had not directly sent him, they had influenced him to act by their attacks on slavery.

The abolitionists did not disavow John Brown. They hailed him as a courageous fighter who had dared to lay hands on a great evil. Emerson and Thoreau and others called him a martyr and saint and compared his execution with the crucifixion of Christ. The gallows on which Brown was hanged was "a stepping stone to heaven," exclaimed Louisa May Alcott. Over and over the abolitionists held up the words in Brown's last testament as a grim prophecy: "I . . . am now quite certain that the crimes of this guilty land will never be purged away but with blood."

The time for blood was not yet come. But on the slavery issue the Northern and Southern peoples were approaching a point of no return. "Shall I tell you what this collision means?" cried William H. Seward for the North in 1858. "It is an irrepressible conflict between opposing and enduring forces, and it means that the United States must and will sooner or later become either entirely a slave-holding nation, or entirely a free labor nation."

"Sir," said Georgia's Alfred Iverson for the South, "disguise the fact as you will, there is an enmity between the Northern and Southern people that is deep and enduring, and you can never eradicate it—never! . . . We are enemies as much as if we were hostile states." In 1860 the nation came to its greatest crisis, and this time there would be no compromise.

AN ESCAPED SLAVE, Margaret Garner is captured in Cincinnati. On the ground lie the bodies of two of her children, whom she was said to have killed so that they would not grow up as slaves. Such incidents roused Northern ire at the Fugitive Slave Act.

The passionate fight to end slavery

SINCE colonial times, there had been protests against slavery in America. But in the years before the Civil War, the drive to end human bondage became a popular and impassioned movement. Fanatical evangelists moved from town to town throughout the North preaching that slavery was a sin and abolition the duty of every Christian. In an era when it was considered improper for women to engage in public activities, a number of women—including the Grimké sisters, abolitionist daughters of a South Carolina slaveholder—made speeches on the slave issue. Thousands of others joined antislavery societies, which were disguised in some border states as sewing circles and library associations.

One of the most striking demonstrations of abolitionist fervor occurred at Lane Theological Seminary in Cincinnati. When antislavery agitation was banned on the campus, virtually the entire student body transferred to Oberlin; that college became a center of the abolitionist movement.

This ferment was brought to a seething climax by three events: a violent reaction to the 1850 Fugitive Slave Act, which required Northerners to return runaway slaves to their masters; the publication of Harriet Beecher Stowe's persuasive antislavery novel *Uncle Tom's Cabin* in 1852; and, at the end of that decade, the plot of John Brown of Kansas (*opposite*) to spark a black revolt by his raid on Harpers Ferry, Virginia. By 1860 America's abolitionists had helped to bring the nation within a step of the battlefield.

FERVENT ABOLITIONIST John Brown roars his defiance in a Kansas torn by the slavery fight. This portrait is from the mural by John Steuart Curry in the Kansas state capitol. Brown's family was riddled with insanity, and many called him mad. "John Brown may be a lunatic," rejoined a Boston paper, but if so "one-fourth of the people of Massachusetts are madmen."

FLEEING SLAVERY, a family rides a stolen horse north to a new life, in this painting by Eastman Johnson. Many ads for fugitives said they had taken cash, clothes and a horse or mule.

"Free seats" to liberty on the Underground Railroad

THE slaves themselves battled bondage in every way they could. They broke tools, ruined crops, set fires and occasionally rebelled. But escape was their best recourse. Although the number who reached freedom was small, hardly an issue of any Southern newspaper appeared without its telltale list of fugitives. Many Negroes fled on foot, traveling at night, sleeping in barns, stealing corn from fields along the road. It took one runaway a year to walk from Alabama to Ohio. Others used fake or stolen "free papers," or rode under freight trains. One slave escaped in style; he disguised his light-skinned wife as a sick "master" who was going north with a servant for treatment. The couple stayed at the best hotels and took the railroad first class.

Many escapees were helped by the Underground Railroad, a loose organization of abolitionists who smuggled fugitives to freedom. The "railroad" even took ads in the newspapers. One read: "The improved and splendid Locomotives . . . will run their regular trips during the present season between . . . the Patriarchal Dominion and Libertyville. . . . SEATS FREE, *irrespective of color."*

ARRIVING SAFELY, weary fugitives enter Levi Coffin's Newport, Indiana, farmyard. When Coffin set up business in the town, near the Ohio border, he learned that local free blacks

were aiding runaways en route to Canada. Then, hearing that some escaped slaves had been retaken because they had been clumsily hidden, Coffin made his own farm into a station of the Underground Railroad. Coffin was later reputed to be "President of the Road." But the work of aiding fugitives was never well enough organized to have "officers," despite the rumors.

The simple story
that "made this big war"

THE tremendous propaganda effect of *Uncle Tom's Cabin*, which at one time ranked next to the Bible in total American sales, was amplified many times over as the story was retold on the stage, on the lecture platform, in the schoolroom. Characters like Little Eva and Simon Legree became the very personifications of good and evil. There were eight different Uncle Tom songs, several dramatic versions, a children's edition and an Uncle Tom card game that "showed the continual separation and reunion of [slave] families." When President Lincoln met Harriet Beecher Stowe in the White House during the Civil War, he was only half joking when he said: "So this is the little lady who made this big war."

A CHILDREN'S VERSION of the book displays Eliza. This volume came out in 1853. In the angry South, children chanted in Richmond streets: "Go, go, go! Ol' Harriet Beecher Stowe!"

A PRINTER'S STAND-BY, this "stock cut" represents Uncle Tom as he was seen on theater programs. From 1852 to 1931 the famous play was never "off the boards" in the United States.

84

A PUBLIC READING is presented by a free black, Mary E. Webb, in England in 1856. A number of London ladies, from Mrs. Charles Dickens to Queen Victoria, were avid readers of Mrs. Stowe's book.

SHEET MUSIC from an 1853 Broadway musical portrays pretty little Cordelia Howard in the part of Eva. Her stage debut, when she was four years old, made her the most popular Eva of the age.

A STAGE PLAY includes a scene not described in the book: Eliza chased by bloodhounds as she crosses the ice. This poster is from a late 19th Century version of the drama. By that time, productions of *Uncle Tom* bore only a vague resemblance to the original; they were often little more than vaudeville shows in which Uncle Tom danced a comic "shuffle and breakdown."

At the moment of defeat, John Brown grips his dying son's hand as Robert E. Lee's troops break into his stronghold at Harpers Ferry.

John Brown's triumphant march to the gallows

WITHOUT the shedding of blood," John Brown once observed, "there is no remission of sins." In Kansas he had cold-bloodedly presided over the butchering of five men in the course of his one-man campaign to end slavery. But it was at Harpers Ferry in 1859 that the fanatical old man brought the purposeful shedding of blood to its ultimate conclusion. In his attack on the Federal arsenal there, he risked his own life and those of his three sons in a gamble he must have known he could not win. When it failed, Brown turned the defeat into a great propaganda triumph, with his own death as the climax. After he was hanged for his crime, he became the North's shining symbol of the fight against human bondage. "That new saint," cried Ralph Waldo Emerson, "... will make the gallows glorious like the Cross." Soon men would be tramping off to war with his name on their lips. "*John Brown's body lies a-mouldering in the grave,*" sang the Union soldiers, "*but his soul goes marching on.*"

AT HIS TRIAL, John Brown lies on a cot in a Virginia courtroom. Brown, wounded in the head and chest by the soldier who captured him, had to be carried into court. He was tried only nine days after the attack and sent to the gallows five weeks later.

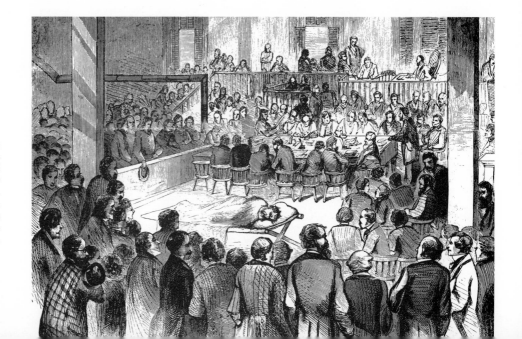

GOING TO HIS DEATH, John Brown is led from jail. This is the scene as the North imagined it. "A black woman with a little child . . . stood by the door," wrote Horace Greeley, who was not there. "He stopped a moment, and stooping, kissed the child." The fact is that none but soldiers met him at the jail; the sorrowing slaves, like Greeley, were present only in spirit.

87

5. SECESSION

I**F** Southern leaders planned it right, William L. Yancey wrote in 1858, "we shall fire the Southern heart—instruct the Southern mind . . . and at the proper moment, by one organized concerted action, we can precipitate the Cotton States into a revolution." When Yancey wrote those ringing words he could feel no certain assurance that his section would take the last great step. The signs he saw were promising, but there were still compromisers who counseled delay.

But now it was 1860 and things were different. Yancey was going to the Democratic Convention as the voice of the Alabama delegation, to present a set of resolutions known as the "Alabama platform." This was ostensibly a proposed platform for the national party, but in reality was much more momentous. It was an ultimatum from the Lower South to the Democrats and to the nation. Alabama was to demand a platform that would, first, affirm the obligation of the federal government to protect slavery in the territories and, second, ratify the principle that the Constitution was merely a compact between the states. If the demand was refused, Alabama would withdraw from the convention.

The delegations of most of the cotton states endorsed the Alabama platform and agreed to follow the bolters. That such a stand would ensure defeat in the election bothered the extreme Southerners not at all. Thus the only remaining national party came to its 1860 convention shaken by serious

INHERITOR OF CRISIS, James Buchanan is remembered for his uncertain actions just before the Civil War. Old and tired, he was trapped by events he could not master.

Vice President John Breckinridge of Kentucky was torn by the sectional split over slavery. Though he ran as the South's candidate for President in 1860, he presided with rigorous impartiality over the tense electoral ballot count that gave Lincoln the election. He was then elected senator, but left to join the Rebel army—and was expelled by the Senate as a traitor.

inner stresses. There were three distinguishable Democratic factions, the Southern, Western and Eastern. The first two constituted major groups and had major objectives, while the weak Eastern faction was interested mainly in patronage rewards. The Western Democrats were in a bitter mood. They resented the rising tempo of Southern attacks on their leader Stephen A. Douglas, and they were impatient with the stubborn Southern opposition to such Western proposals as a homestead bill and internal improvements. But they wanted to win the coming election. Committed to popular sovereignty, they were nevertheless willing to accept some vague, face-saving platform that both major factions could live with. On two issues they would yield nothing: the party could not carry the key Northern states, and hence the election, with any candidate but Douglas; and the adoption of Yancey's slave code for the territories would guarantee the defeat of any candidate.

THE Democratic Convention met in Charleston in April. The stately old city was always lovely and especially so in spring. It had much to charm visitors, especially those from a more severe climate—gardens rioting with azaleas, camellias and roses; majestic churches that recalled the age of Christopher Wren; spacious houses fronting toward the Battery wall and the sea breezes. But for all its outward attractions the metropolis of South Carolina was the last place where men of diverse views on slavery might discuss their differences calmly. The political center of the states' rights movement, the city was also in a real and recognized sense the cultural capital of the South. John C. Calhoun slept in St. Philip's churchyard, but his spirit still walked the streets and his voice still spoke in the words of younger disciples.

Charleston did not have the physical accommodations to handle a large convention. The two best hotels, the Mills House and the Charleston House, could take care of only a fraction of the delegates, even by assigning five or six men to a room. The Pennsylvania, Massachusetts and New York delegations arrived on steamboats, which they expected to use as floating hotels but which became prohibitively expensive as the convention continued in session longer than anticipated. The Douglas delegations from the Northwest rented Hibernia Hall and stuffed 132 cots on a single floor.

Many of the visitors brought along copious stocks of stimulants, but these did not survive the prolonged sessions. "A great calamity has come upon the Ohio delegation," reported one journalist. "Their private whiskey, of which they laid in a supply supposed to be equal to all emergencies, the nomination of Douglas included, gave out this morning." Even the weather worked against the Democrats. It was unseasonably hot, in the 90s, when the convention opened; then it rained and turned cold.

The whole atmosphere of the city was hostile to Northerners. Because of this hostility, the high prices, and the difficulty of securing lodgings, many visitors left. As a result, the galleries were packed with howling supporters of the extreme Southern position. Moderate Southerners who ordinarily might have taken a sober second look at some propositions were swept along by the rolling applause and acted more extremely than they intended.

The convention immediately took on the aspects of a dramatic conflict. The first test of strength came over the platform plank on slavery and the territories. The resolutions committee, reflecting the division in the party, presented three proposals. One, offered by the Southerners, declared that the federal government had an obligation to protect slavery in the territories. A second, put forward by Benjamin F. Butler of Massachusetts, merely reaffirmed the doctrine of popular sovereignty. The third plank proposed, the Western, also endorsed popular sovereignty, but stated in addition that all questions involving rights to slave property in the states or territories should be referred to the Supreme Court. This last plank said practically nothing, which was the intention of its framers. It was designed to hold the party together by means of an evasion and to enable it to win the election.

Ordinarily politicians would eagerly embrace such a compromise. It was a mark of the extraordinary times that the Southerners could no longer act as politicians—to them principle, dogma, had become more important than adjustment and party success. In a heated floor debate on the three proposed planks they demanded their way or threatened to walk out.

Then for the galleries and the extreme Southerners the great moment came. Yancey rose to a storm of applause and a shower of flowers. The South would stand on principle even if the party had to be defeated, he announced. As the excitement of the audience mounted, he flung out his defiance: "Ours is the property invaded; ours are the institutions which are at stake; ours is the peace that is to be destroyed; ours is the honor at stake . . . we yield no position here until we are convinced we are wrong!"

The gas lamps had been lit that night when Ohio's George E. Pugh rose to reply for the Northwest. Pugh knew he faced a hostile audience, but he was too infuriated to care. In words as measured and as uncompromising as Yancey's he cried: "The Northern Democrats are not children, to be told to stand here—to stand there—to be moved at the beck and bidding of the South . . . we are told, in effect, that we must put our hands on our mouths, and our mouths in the dust. Gentlemen of the South, you mistake us—you mistake us!—*We will not do it!*"

The convention was now in such an uproar that no vote could be taken, and the managers adjourned it until the next day, Saturday—and then again to Monday. Over the Sabbath moderate men worked to effect a compromise. None was forthcoming, and those who could still think clearly realized that the historic Democratic party was on the verge of dissolution.

On Monday, April 30, the convention presented a confused scene. The Douglas forces pushed through a plank reaffirming popular sovereignty. All over the hall men were on their feet shouting angry words. Suddenly the din hushed as the chairman of the Alabama delegation gained the floor. He announced that pursuant to instructions Alabama was leaving the convention. As the Alabamians walked out they were followed by some or all of the delegates from seven other states. The galleries roared their approval, but on the convention floor men watched in stunned silence, aware that they were looking on something too serious to cheer about.

Mocking Stephen A. Douglas' vain effort to suit all factions at the 1860 Democratic Convention, held in Charleston, this cartoon—captioned "Dancing for Eels in the Charleston Market"—shows the Little Giant striving to please while other Democrats watch disapprovingly. The frowning party chiefs include President Buchanan (left) and Jefferson Davis (right).

T HE Southern departure left the remaining delegates in a sad quandary. To the dismay of the Douglas backers, a resolution was adopted declaring that the nominee had to attain a two thirds vote of the total number of delegates, including the bolters. One delegate said the decision had the sound of clods falling on the Little Giant's coffin. In the voting that followed, Douglas led on 57 ballots but he could not mount the strength to win. In frustration the convention adjourned, to reconvene in Baltimore on June 18. The Southern bolters also called a convention of their own to meet in Richmond on June 11.

But time produced no healing effect. On the contrary, attitudes hardened. At Baltimore many Southerners reappeared, but when the credentials of some were questioned they walked out again. Meeting in another hall, the seceders nominated John C. Breckinridge of Kentucky as their candidate. The Charleston bolters meeting at Richmond endorsed his selection. Those who stayed in the original Baltimore meeting finally nominated Douglas.

Both groups called themselves Democrats, and each professed to represent the true faith. But nothing could disguise the fact that there now were two Democratic parties, Northern and Southern. The division augured a Republican victory in the election.

Senator John Bell voted more like a Northerner than a Tennessean. Risking his constituents' wrath, he backed the abolitionists' right of petition, resisted the Kansas-Nebraska Act and opposed slavery in the capital. Yet when he ran for President he was the only candidate to carry his home county.

T HE Republicans gathered that May, with fitting symbolism, in the booming, bustling Western metropolis of Chicago. If time seemed to stand still in Charleston, in Chicago it moved with revolutionary rapidity. From a population of 250 in 1832 the city had soared to almost 110,000 in 1860. To house the convention Chicago had characteristically erected a special building, a huge wooden structure called the Wigwam, capable of holding 10,000 people. Chicagoans bragged that it was the largest auditorium in the country. It seemed to burst with spectators and enthusiasm at every session. As at Charleston, the galleries were a part of the convention and at the right moment would communicate their emotions to the delegates.

Although the Republicans sniffed victory, behind the scenes the managers and the leaders were moving with cool precision. Their task was delicate. A new Republican image had to be created—of a conservative party that represented several ideas rather than merely one and that stood *for* things as well as being against something. The platform that was finally adopted appealed to every major power group in the North; it combined the antislavery impulse with the economic aspirations of the region. The Republicans reaffirmed their unalterable opposition to slavery's expansion. They also promised a protective tariff, internal improvements, a homestead bill and a Pacific railroad.

Hannibal Hamlin, elected Vice President in 1860, was so swarthy many Southerners insisted he was a Negro; three derisive South Carolinians wrote Lincoln offering to buy Hamlin as a slave. He was never close to the President; like other Vice Presidents he protested: "I am not consulted at all."

The same careful, conservative approach was exhibited in the choice of a candidate. The contender with the most preconvention delegates was William H. Seward, and behind him came Salmon P. Chase and a batch of minor aspirants. But Seward and Chase were impossible candidates in an election where victory was possible. Both were too prominent. They had said too many things too many times and offended too many blocs of voters. The convention managers needed a different kind of candidate. He had to be from a large state, to possess some reputation and to be a firm antislavery man but not an extremist. Only one man fitted the specifications. At an early date the stop-Seward forces settled on Abraham Lincoln of Illinois, favorite of the galleries.

That Seward and Lincoln were the chief contenders became evident once the candidates were put in nomination. At the mention of Seward's name his supporters emitted a mighty blast. "The effect was startling," wrote one reporter. "Hundreds of persons stopped their ears in pain. The shouting was absolutely frantic, shrill and wild." But, unbelievably, the Lincoln legions, aided by the galleries, did even better. "The uproar was beyond description," recorded the same reporter.

Two hundred thirty-three votes were necessary for a choice. On the first ballot Seward led with 173½ votes and Lincoln had 102. But Lincoln gained on the second ballot and won on the third. Hannibal Hamlin of Maine, a former Democrat, was nominated for second place on the ticket.

The Republicans and the two groups of Democrats were not the only parties to offer candidates. A fourth party was organized calling itself the Constitutional Union party. Its creators were conservative elder statesmen who felt that a victory for any one of the major parties would serve to heighten sectional discord. By putting forward their own candidates, they hoped to scatter the electoral vote so that no party would secure a majority, and thus to throw the election into the House of Representatives, where a conservative might be chosen. Their nominees were John Bell of Tennessee and Edward Everett of Massachusetts, and their platform declared simply for the Constitution and the Union. Ridiculed as the "Old Gentlemen's" or the "Do-Nothing" party, they were moderate men with patriotic impulses who did not quite understand what was happening to their country.

The campaign revealed ominously the disruptive influence of sectionalism on the normal workings of American politics. The familiar features were present—rallies, parades and speeches. But there was something strangely different. Essentially the contest developed into a struggle of parties within sections. In the North it was Lincoln against Douglas; in the South, Breckinridge against Bell or Douglas. No one of the four parties developed significant strength on a national scale.

The two Democratic factions attacked each other with concentrated virulence. A Republican leader, observing their feud in Pennsylvania, remarked elatedly, "The Douglas and Breckinridge men would give it to us to spite each other." Supporters of Breckinridge and Bell vied as to which man would better uphold Southern rights. The Republicans emphasized the economic benefits their program would confer on the North. Why, said Seward at Dubuque, Iowa, "there is no Negro question about it at all. It is an eternal question between classes—between the few privileged and the many unprivileged—the eternal question between aristocracy and democracy."

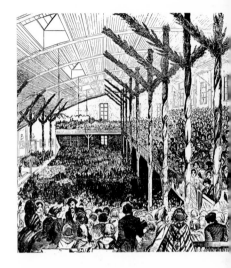

The Republican convention hall in Chicago is jammed with noisy spectators. A contemporary described the bedlam this crowd created as Abraham Lincoln won the nomination: "A thousand steam whistles, ten acres of hotel gongs, a tribe of Comanches might have mingled in the scene unnoticed."

IN all the shouting few noted or took seriously threats from leaders in the Deep South that their section would secede if the Republicans won the election. One of those who did take notice was Douglas. As the campaign progressed, sensing defeat for himself and fearing the results of a Republican victory, he embarked on a speaking tour of the South. He exhorted Southerners to accept the outcome of the election, no matter what it was, and warned that the North would never permit the Union to be destroyed. He minced no words. At Raleigh he told a frigid audience: "I would hang every man higher than Haman who would attempt to resist by force the execution of any provision of the Constitution which our fathers made and bequeathed to us." It was a selfless action by a great politician. His arduous speechmaking contributed to the exhaustion that helped bring about his death within a year.

The election on November 6 disclosed to the country a Republican victory. Lincoln won the presidency, although his party did not win control of Congress. (By the time he took office, however, the secession of the Democratic South had given the Republicans a majority in both Houses.) The distribution of votes was revealing. Lincoln had 180 electoral votes, a clear majority, and 1,866,000 popular votes or 40 per cent of the total. Douglas stood second in popular votes, with 1,383,000, but he was lowest in electoral votes, with 12.

Breckinridge had 72 electoral and 848,000 popular votes; Bell, 39 and 593,000. Lincoln carried every free state except New Jersey, and even here he had four electoral votes and Douglas three. Breckinridge took every state in the Lower South plus North Carolina, Delaware and Maryland. Bell won the border states of Tennessee, Kentucky and Virginia. Douglas secured only Missouri, in addition to the three New Jersey votes.

IT is possible to place different interpretations on the meaning of the election, and many have been advanced. But surely the most portentous analysis was the one arrived at immediately by the South: the election had turned in every way against the minority section.

It was bad enough, Southerners felt, that a sectional party hostile to Southern interests had elected its candidate to the highest office in the land. The ultimate danger was even greater. Lincoln and Douglas, both committed by one formula or another to excluding slavery from the territories, had together amassed approximately 70 per cent of the total vote. An unmistakable majority had declared that the South's peculiar institution must be penned up where it was and thus placed on the road to eventual extinction. It was a decision the South believed it could not ignore.

In the Lower South men were ready with an answer. They had long known what they must do if, in their revealing language, "the enemy" won control of the government. The South must secede. "Let the consequences be what they may," declared an Atlanta paper, "whether the Potomac is crimsoned in human gore, and Pennsylvania Avenue is paved ten fathoms deep with mangled bodies or whether the last vestige of liberty is swept from the face of the American Continent, the South will never submit to such humiliation and degradation as the inauguration of Abraham Lincoln."

Those Southerners who favored secession cried that it must be put through in the four months between the November election and Lincoln's ascension to the presidency in March of 1861. "Twenty years of labor and toil and taxes all expended upon preparation," thundered Georgia's Toombs, "would not make up for the advantage your enemies would gain if the rising sun on the fifth of March should find you in the Union."

Not all Southerners favored immediate secession; some felt that the mere election of a Republican President did not justify hasty action. But though they proposed some more moderate alternatives, their cause was almost hopeless. In the cities crowds surged in the streets to hear fiery speeches from extremist leaders and to shout for independence, and in some places the national flag went down and the state flag went up. "People are wild," wrote a South Carolina politician. "The scenes of the French Revolution are being enacted already. . . . God knows the end." A secessionist observer thought that the people were ahead of the politicians. "You might as well attempt to control a tornado as to attempt to stop them from secession," he reported. The people might be ahead of some politicians, but they were just catching up with the ultrasecessionists, the Yanceys, Rhetts and others. These men were now riding the crest, and they were as intoxicated by the heady atmosphere as the masses. In fact, secession unfolded like a thrilling adventure. Men had the sense of participating in a moment of destiny, and they acted with eager joy.

Between the dates of Lincoln's election in November and the first of February seven Deep South states held conventions and voted to secede. They

This slyly ambiguous clothing ad, combining business acumen with good secessionist sentiment, ran in the Charleston "Courier" before the result of the 1860 election was known. Many in South Carolina thought Lincoln a "vulgar mobocrat and Southern hater" who would "force amalgamation between [Negroes] and the children of the poor men of the South."

were, in the order of their leaving, South Carolina, Mississippi, Florida, Alabama, Georgia, Louisiana and Texas. The South Carolina convention acted by a unanimous vote, and in the Mississippi and Florida meetings the opposition was slight. But in the important states of Alabama and Georgia, there was much moderate sentiment; in their conventions measures offered by proponents of delay narrowly missed passage. When the decision was known in Georgia, Herschel V. Johnson, who had run for Vice President on the Douglas ticket and had opposed secession, recorded sentiments which revealed that some Southerners viewed the dissolution of the Union not with joy, but with an infinite grief. "And so the Rubicon was crossed," Johnson wrote, "and the State of Georgia was launched upon a dark, uncertain and dangerous sea. The secessionists were jubilant. I never felt so sad before." Louisiana and Texas voted to secede by a substantial majority.

With flashing fervor and confident determination, and also with some reluctance, the cotton South had at last left the Union. It had left because it felt its interests were no longer safe. But its leaders knew that their people could have no future existing as separate states. From the beginning the plan had been that after the departure was accomplished the South would create its own political association, a new nation founded on the great principle of states' rights. In February delegates from the seceded states met at Montgomery, Alabama, and founded a new nation. They called it the Confederate States of America, and as its first President they chose Jefferson Davis.

SECESSION forced on another President his cruelest crisis. With great hesitation and without much dignity, James Buchanan still faced up to events. In his message to Congress of December 3, delivered before any state had seceded but when preparations were being openly made, he spoke compellingly of the might and the perpetuity of the American government. He denied that a state could lawfully leave the Union, but he added that it was doubtful if the government had the power to force a seceded state to return to the Union.

The contradiction in his thinking—a state could not secede but nobody could stop it—was widely ridiculed. There was, however, some purpose in his apparent confusion. He was doing all that he felt he could. Even if he had been disposed to use force, he had little to employ; the small regular army of less than 15,000 was scattered at many posts, mostly in the West. Nor was it certain that at this stage Northern opinion would support a show of force. The North had watched with unbelieving eyes as the secession adventure unfolded. It could not believe as yet that disruption was real; its every inclination was to maintain the Union, even by coercion if necessary, but the fact of secession had first to be realized before opinion would sanction action.

Buchanan's policy was to confine secession to as few states as possible and then hand the problem over to Lincoln and the Republicans. But when the procession of seceding states continued despite his conciliatory attitude, he was hurt and fussily irritated, and slowly his opposition to secession stiffened. At all times he maintained the symbolic authority of the government. He maintained it with special firmness in regard to federal property. This was an area where its loss might have been fatal—where, if he had yielded, the whole concept of the Union might have shattered.

The states, as they seceded, had taken possession of federal properties within their borders. But two installations they could not seize immediately

CHARLESTON MERCURY EXTRA:

Passed unanimously at 1.15 o'clock, P. M. December 20th, 1860.

AN ORDINANCE

To dissolve the Union between the State of South Carolina and other States united with her under the compact entitled "The Constitution of the United States of America."

THE UNION IS DISSOLVED!

South Carolinians greeted secession with jubilation. Charleston, one observer noted, "... was wild with excitement ... church bells mingling with salvos of artillery. ... Old men ran shouting down the street.... The whole heart of the people had spoken." But a lonely Unionist said sourly: "South Carolina is too small for a republic and too big for a lunatic asylum."

for want of naval strength: Fort Sumter in Charleston harbor and Fort Pickens off Florida's coast at Pensacola. Sumter, held by a small garrison of 75 men under Major Robert Anderson, immediately became, because of its relation to South Carolina, a focal point of national interest. South Carolina sent commissioners to Washington to negotiate for the transfer of the fort—the nation of South Carolina offering to treat with the nation of the United States —but Buchanan, although he received the commissioners unofficially, refused to yield the fort. In his rising anger at the disunionists, he even tried to strengthen the garrison. He sent to Sumter in January an unarmed steamer, the *Star of the West*, with troops and supplies. At the entrance to the harbor South Carolina military forces fired on the vessel and turned her back. It was an act of war, but no outraged burst of patriotism shook the North.

A lifelong maverick, Texas Governor Sam Houston was a Southerner who supported the Union. He prevented the state legislature from voting for secession—and when secession was approved by the voters he refused to swear allegiance to the Confederacy. He retired to his farm and died there in 1863.

As this first act of the Sumter drama was being played, Congress was busily trying to devise some scheme of compromise in the tradition of the great adjustment of 1850. Both chambers appointed committees to study possible plans. Of the propositions submitted by these groups, that of the Senate committee commanded major attention. Framed by Kentucky's venerable John J. Crittenden, regarded as the heir of Henry Clay, it became known as the Crittenden Compromise. It recommended a series of constitutional amendments which would have guaranteed the existence of slavery in those states where it was already established and would have satisfied Southern demands on such grievances as fugitive slaves.

Crittenden boldly tried to settle the key issue, the one on which the fate of any compromise would hang, the status of slavery in the territories. He proposed to restore the Missouri Compromise line as a dividing border between freedom and slavery in all territories then held or thereafter acquired. The Southern members of the committee indicated that they would accept this arrangement if the Republican members would approve it. The Republicans felt that they should sound out President-elect Lincoln in Springfield. Lincoln advised rejection. To divide the territories on a line, he said, would dilute the party platform and encourage the South to embark on land-grabbing adventures in Latin America. The Republican senators obeyed his wishes—and the committee had to announce to the Senate that it had no plan.

John Crittenden of Kentucky, who tried to pacify North and South with his compromise, was another Southerner with divided sympathies. He said, "I must still regard seceders countrymen," but stayed a Union senator during the war. One son fought as a Confederate general, another as a Northerner.

The House committee, like the Senate body, foundered on the territorial question. The committee Republicans voted down the Missouri Compromise line proposal, and the Southerners would accept nothing less.

Also ending in failure was the one attempt made outside Congress to devise a compromise. Virginia, one of the slave states that had not yet seceded, invited the other states to send delegates to a peace conference at Washington in early February. Twenty-one states attended, and the gathering, known as the Peace Convention, labored for weeks to produce a plan. It finally came up with a measure that practically duplicated Crittenden's scheme but tried to meet Republican objections to the Missouri line—it stipulated that no territory could be acquired by the United States thereafter without the consent of a majority of senators from both sections. Laid before Congress on the eve of Lincoln's inauguration, it was rejected without serious consideration.

While men labored in and out of Congress to effect a compromise, Abraham Lincoln left Springfield for Washington. Because it was thought necessary that the President-elect show himself throughout the North, Lincoln traveled a long, roundabout route that consumed 11 days and took him through five states. There were countless receptions, and on every occasion Lincoln was called on for a speech. Nearly always he responded. In these remarks he was not in his best form. He could not reveal his policy on secession, he did not want to alarm the country with grim predictions and he had to talk too many times. Therefore he spoke in a light and ordinary vein, and he seemed to be frivolous and unaware of the crisis. Other incidents added to the picture of a man unequal to his task. In a little Pennsylvania town a coal miner yelled that he did not think Lincoln was taller than he. Obligingly the President-elect invited him up the platform to measure, and before the crowd the two men stood back to back. At Westfield, New York, Lincoln called to the rear platform of his train an 11-year-old girl named Grace Bedell. He revealed that during the campaign she had written him that he would look much handsomer if he grew some whiskers. He said, "You see, I let these whiskers grow for you, Grace," and kissed the child. He attended the opera in New York City and violated social custom by wearing black gloves instead of white. Correct society shuddered at the prospect of such a man in the White House.

In Philadelphia a private detective, Allan Pinkerton, came to Lincoln with disquieting news. Pinkerton said he had certain intelligence that Southern sympathizers in Baltimore, where Lincoln had to change train stations, would try to kill the President-elect. Lincoln was inclined to dismiss the report as a rumor. But soon Frederick Seward, son of the senator, arrived. His father had heard the same story and wanted Lincoln to take precautions. Against his better judgment, Lincoln allowed himself to be persuaded. He went on to Harrisburg to attend a ceremony and then submitted to a scheme concocted by his friends, railroad officials and Pinkerton. Leaving Harrisburg secretly by train on February 22, he transferred at Philadelphia to a sleeper, taking a berth reserved by a female Pinkerton operator for her "invalid brother." The party passed safely through Baltimore at 3:30 in the morning and reached Washington at 6 a.m. on the 23rd. The elated Pinkerton sent a code note to Harrisburg: "Plums Delivered Nuts Safely."

The secret dash aroused wide ridicule. The President-elect had slunk into Washington, cried the Democratic and Southern press. During the journey Lincoln had carried a shawl to drape over his shoulders, and out of this arose a tale that he had worn some kind of disguise. The cruelest gibes came from the South. A Richmond editor spoke of the "Abolition orang-outang that skulked to Washington the other day from the wilds of Illinois, and who will, in three days more, be propped in the Chair of Washington by the sword of a military dictator." The whole episode revealed how men were losing their grip on reality. Whether or not there was a plot to kill Lincoln is still unknown. He himself doubted there was and always regretted that he had given way to his excited advisers. The Richmond journalist's military dictator who was going to inaugurate Lincoln by force was General Winfield Scott, commanding general of the Army, who had at his disposal not more than 900 men.

WHEN Lincoln assumed the presidency on March 4, Buchanan's policy of drift and compromise had had four months of trial. It had permitted the secession of seven slave states and the formation of a new and confident Southern nation. Still the eight slave states of the Upper and Border South had remained in the Union. Would a continuation of the same policy avert

In Scottish bonnet, Lincoln peers from a train in a cartoon ridiculing his incognito arrival in Washington for his inauguration. Warned of a plot in proslavery Baltimore to assassinate him, the President-elect did sneak through the Maryland city at night, but the disguise shown here was a reporter's invention.

further secessions and isolate the cotton states and compel their eventual return? Or would it result in the permanent division of the Union? The country waited anxiously to see what Lincoln's policy would be.

Lincoln announced his policy in his inaugural address, the first of the great state papers that would come from his pen. In a pronouncement dealing with such a sensitive situation no reasonably adept politician would reveal every detail of his program. Lincoln was more than adept; he was a superb politician. He deliberately obscured some of his intentions, and he left himself some possible loopholes. Still he outlined with essential clarity his views of the current crisis.

The Union was older than the states and was founded for perpetuity, he said; secession was an illegal and revolutionary act. In the immediate situation he would proceed with forbearance and caution for a period, but he would endeavor to enforce federal laws in all the states and he would retain possession of federal property—by which he meant Sumter and Pickens.

No threat to the constitutional rights of the secessionist states was contemplated; and if the seceded states wished to return they could—but without exacting any conditions. Then, although still employing velvet language, Lincoln showed a hint of the iron in him. The government would act to defend itself, he asserted, and here he spoke directly to the South: "In *your* hands, my dissatisfied fellow countrymen, and not in *mine*, is the momentous issue of civil war. The government will not assail *you*. You can have no conflict, without being yourselves the aggressors. *You* have no oath registered in Heaven to destroy the government, while *I* shall have the most solemn one to 'preserve, protect and defend it.'" And he ended with a moving passage:

"I am loath to close. We are not enemies, but friends. We must not be enemies. Though passion may have strained, it must not break our bonds of affection. The mystic chords of memory, stretching from every battlefield, and patriot grave, to every living heart and hearthstone, all over this broad land, will yet swell the chorus of the Union, when again touched, as surely they will be, by the better angels of our nature."

Buchanan (left) and Lincoln ride toward the Capitol for Lincoln's inauguration. An observer noted: "The . . . pallid face and perfectly white hair of Mr. Buchanan contrasted powerfully with the tall figure, coal-black hair and rugged features of Mr. Lincoln and suggested that the exhausted energies of the old were to be followed by the vigorous strength of the new."

POSSIBLY Lincoln meant to experiment for a brief period with a policy of coaxing conciliation, but fate took the initiative away from him. Right after his inauguration he learned that Major Anderson's men were running out of provisions and unless supplied would have to evacuate Fort Sumter.

In Lincoln's thinking, to lose Sumter would be to lose a vital symbol of national authority. After painful deliberation, he decided to send a naval relief expedition to Charleston. Carefully avoiding any dealings with the Confederacy, he informed the South Carolina authorities that the expedition was on the way. His decision to relieve the fort placed the Confederate government in a situation from which there was no escape. If it permitted the ships to land, then replenished Sumter could hold out indefinitely. The new Southern government would be in the impossible position of bowing to federal power and of permitting the fort of another nation to command one of its principal harbors. But the hard alternative was to attack and reduce Sumter before the relief force arrived—in short, to start a war.

This was what the men at Montgomery, after anguished discussion, decided to do. Orders went out to the Confederate commander at Charleston, Louisiana's dashing Creole soldier, General P.G.T. Beauregard, to demand the surrender of the installation and, if the demand was refused, to reduce the fort by arms. Beauregard served his summons, Anderson rejected it and on April 12 the Confederate guns opened on the fort. They fired all that day and into the night, and on the next day the helpless garrison yielded.

The fall of Fort Sumter threw the North into a frenzy of outraged patriotism. All doubts and divisions dissolved at the news that the flag had been fired on. A near-unanimous public voice demanded punishment of the perpetrators and the preservation of the Union by whatever force was required. "Fort Sumter is lost, but freedom is saved," rejoiced the New York *Tribune*. "There is no more thought of bribing or coaxing the traitors who have dared to aim their cannon balls at the flag of the Union, and those who gave their lives to defend it. . . . Fort Sumter is temporarily lost, but the country is saved. Live the Republic!"

Lincoln called on the states for 75,000 volunteers to deal with certain "combinations too powerful to be suppressed by the ordinary course of judicial proceedings." He did not say so, but everybody knew that the country was now at war.

THE situation posed a problem for the states of the Upper South. Committed to the doctrine of state sovereignty and bound culturally to the cotton states, they had considered secession before Sumter but had decided Lincoln's election was not sufficient reason to act. But if the national government could coerce states back into the Union, state sovereignty would become a mere empty phrase. Not enthusiastically but with settled determination, four more states—Virginia, Arkansas, Tennessee and North Carolina—seceded and joined the Confederacy. Even at this stage four slave states remained in the Union—Missouri, Kentucky, Maryland and Delaware. They were divided in sentiment and sympathy but, although pressure from the national government played some part in influencing their decision, their fundamental devotion was to the Union.

The crisis of 1860-1861 was a unique episode in the American record. It is the only time that the most pragmatic people in Western civilization have been unable to adjust their differences by the normal political method of compromise, the only time that a defeated minority felt it could not live with its defeat, the only time that a domestic dispute was referred to the arbitration of war.

The secession crisis, which was the climax of the sectional controversy, and the Civil War, which was the culmination of the secession crisis—together they represent the one great American failure, the one great national tragedy. The tragedy did not strike the country simply because men were fanatical or selfish or shortsighted, although some men were all of these. Its origins were embedded in the American ethic and the American dream, and it burst forth when people became aroused over an abstract moral issue and related that issue to all their other differences.

There may have been a time when the North and the South could have adjusted their disputes, could have achieved a solution even for the problem of slavery. If so, that moment passed by before men realized it was gone, lost somewhere in the winds of debate. Then it was too late. The American people for once, as other peoples have many times, lost control of their destiny. "And the war came," said Abraham Lincoln. Perhaps it had always been inevitable.

Louisianian Pierre G. T. Beauregard, depicted as a play-acting cavalier in this cartoon, was superintendent of West Point when his state seceded. Reluctant to give up that coveted post, the future Rebel general claimed he could perform his duties even while loyal to Louisiana. But he was asked to resign—and he then billed the U.S. for fare home. He never collected.

A man on the road to immortality

ON April 15, 1837, a gawky lawyer, riding a borrowed horse with all his belongings in two saddlebags, arrived in Springfield, Illinois *(below)*, to open a law office. He was Abraham Lincoln, 28 and at the mid-point of his life: 28 years later, to the day, he would die at an assassin's hand.

In the Springfield years Lincoln pioneered as a corporation lawyer for the new railroads and the canal companies, making fees of up to $5,000 (that was from the Illinois Central, and he had to sue to collect). He also practiced in small-town courts, ranging the countryside in his buggy with his legal papers tucked into his frayed silk hat. He met and charmed people all over the state, and built a political following that sent him to Washington in 1847 for a single term as congressman *(opposite)*.

But he was not yet ready for greatness. He returned to Springfield to work out his personal philosophy, sometimes in lonely introspection, sometimes reading newspapers aloud—to the annoyance of his partner, William H. Herndon. For Lincoln, those years were invaluable. In 1861, leaving Springfield forever, he said: "To this place and the kindness of these people I owe everything."

A YOUNG CAPITAL, Springfield had been seat of the state government only a few months when Lincoln opened a law office (1). He and Herndon later shared an office (2) down the street.

A YOUNG POLITICIAN, Representative Lincoln *(right)* displays the powerful physique of the frontiersman in this picture, his first known portrait, taken around the time of his election.

A FRIENDLY CARTOON pokes fun at Lincoln's reputation as a rail splitter. The caption said: "A 'Rail' Old Western Gentleman." Most 1860 cartoons on the subject were far more scathing.

Little did I think when I split these rails, that they would be the means of elevating me to my present position.

REPUBLICAN PLATFORM.

AN OPPOSITION SKETCH portrays the presidential candidate atop a woodpile within which a Negro finds shelter. Despite the legend on the rail, the party platform did not favor abolition.

A ROMANTICIZED PAINTING depicts The Rail Splitter in his youth. In the background is a flatboat of the sort Lincoln once worked on. The canvas probably was shown at political rallies.

A prairie candidate with faith that "right makes might"

W HEN Lincoln rose to speak at New York's Cooper Union in February 1860, he seemed to many an unlikely presidential prospect. At 51, his highest office had been that one term in Congress; since then, his political record had consisted mainly of two senatorial defeats. His ill-fitting suit was rumpled; his new shoes hurt his feet. His manner of speech bore traces of the frontier, and at first the audience was embarrassed for him. But his words swiftly gripped them, and they applauded warmly. When he had finished ("Let us have faith that right makes might, and in that faith, let us, to the end, dare to do our duty"), he was a major contender *(right)*.

His nomination was clinched that spring when his supporters paraded through the convention hall carrying two of the 3,000 fence rails they said he had split as a youth. The image of The Rail Splitter fired the public imagination. On election night, the story goes, Lincoln rushed home to tell his wife: "Mary, we're elected!"

THE CANDIDATE appears in this photograph taken by Mathew Brady the day of the Cooper speech. When Brady moved his collar, Lincoln said, "Ah, I see you want to shorten my neck."

THE CANDIDATE'S HOME is shown in this campaign photograph. Lincoln and two sons, Willie and Tad, stand behind the fence; the blurred figure in front is a neighbor's child. Lincoln often pulled the boys in a wagon up and down this street. Occasionally they fell out, and he, deep in thought, went on. Lincoln bought the house for $1,500; he added the second story.

103

REVIEWING VOLUNTEERS, Lincoln stands in a pavilion raised before the White House. He often recalled that he too had been a volunteer—in the Black Hawk War of 1832. Once he had to march his militiamen through a narrow gate. Unable to think of the right order, he commanded: "This company will break ranks and re-form immediately on the other side."

Lincoln confronts McClellan at Antietam. When "Little Mac" wrote later that his horses were tired, Lincoln retorted: "Will you pardon

A wartime leader
with problems of command

Of all Lincoln's burdens as Commander in Chief, few caused him more concern than his generals. He carried on an increasingly desperate search for just one good commander; the hunt lasted until the emergence of U. S. Grant in 1864. During those years the Army of the Potomac, charged with guarding Washington and destroying the Confederates in the East, had six different leaders; these men piled missed opportunity on top of near disaster until Lincoln was frantic.

Of them all, none showed more promise or gave more trouble than George B. McClellan (*below*). A superb horseman, he dashed boldly about Washington, but at the front he was strangely cautious. He consistently overestimated enemy strength and refused to attack without reinforcements. Sending troops to McClellan was like shoveling fleas across a barnyard, said Lincoln; so few seemed to get there. McClellan was the only general to get a second chance—and he failed both times.

THE COMMANDER IN CHIEF reveals the strain of leadership in 1862. He told a friend that year: "It appears to me the Almighty is against us, and I can hardly see a ray of hope."

me for asking what the horses of your army have done . . . that fatigues anything?"

WITH A DETESTED GENERAL, Lincoln appears in this Rebel cartoon as Don Quixote to Benjamin F. Butler's Sancho Panza. Southerners hated Butler for his occupation of New Orleans; Northerners accused him of corruption.

105

WITH HIS OPPONENT, McClellan, the Democratic candidate in 1864, Lincoln is an amused giant in this *Harper's* cartoon. McClellan's spade suggests his army did nothing but dig in.

WITH HIS OFFICIALS, Lincoln and his wife are surrounded by Cabinet members and officers at a reception. Once, while he was handshaking, Lincoln's kid glove burst with a loud pop.

WITH HIS FAMILY, Lincoln appears in a lithograph. Actually, Robert Todd was not yet in uniform when Willie, beside his father, died. Mary rests a hand on Tad's shoulder.

Behind the public image
"a furnace of affliction"

LINCOLN was devoted to his family, but his personal life as President is summed up in a phrase his wife, Mary, used to describe her own life at this time: "a furnace of affliction." She was speaking of the tragedy of 11-year-old Willie's death in 1862. For Lincoln, there was also the more subtle tragedy of Mary's growing mental illness. She could be a gracious hostess, but she had tantrums with the servants and quarrels with Cabinet wives. Her shopping sprees became notorious. Once she overspent a $20,000 appropriation for White House furnishings by $7,000—then tried to hush up the debt.

Through it all, Lincoln stood by her. When senators charged she was a spy, he defended her at a secret hearing. For her part, even when she was most difficult, she sustained him—coaxing him to eat his breakfast egg, taking him for a daily drive—through the war, through re-election, to final victory. In her wedding ring was engraved: "Love is eternal." For the Lincolns, it was true.

A WAR-WEARY LEADER, Lincoln reveals stress in this photograph taken a few days before he delivered the Gettysburg Address in 1863. It is the best-known full-face portrait of Lincoln.

WITH HIS SON Tad, Lincoln strolls through Richmond, the fallen Confederate capital, in April 1865. Negroes cheered the President, but officials were deeply concerned for his safety.

107

"Unspeakable peace" for a martyred President

ON April 14, 1865, Good Friday, five days after Lee's surrender, Lincoln and his wife drove out from the White House for one of the President's rare evenings of relaxation. "I never felt so happy in my life," he had told Mary that afternoon. Now they were going with two young people, Clara Harris and her fiancé, Major Henry Rathbone, to see an English comedy, *Our American Cousin*, at Ford's Theater. And there, as they watched, John Wilkes Booth slipped into the presidential box, leveled a derringer at Lincoln's head and fired a shot (*below*). Then he leaped to the stage and fled.

Lincoln died at 7:22 the next morning—on his face, as one witness said, "a look of unspeakable peace." A funeral train of seven cars bore his body north through New York, then westward to Chicago and home to Springfield. There were throngs of mourners in the cities, and all along the 1,700-mile route countryfolk lined the tracks with bonfires at night or stood in the cold spring rain, holding out bouquets, as the train crept by. Silently, they echoed the aged Negro woman in Philadelphia who had laid a bough on the coffin and cried: "Oh, Abraham Lincoln, are you dead? Are you dead?"

LINCOLN'S ASSASSINATION is portrayed in this Currier & Ives print: as Booth fires, Rathbone (*left*) tries to intervene. Booth was later hunted down by troops; he died of a bullet wound.

LINCOLN'S LAST PHOTOGRAPH, in which he wears a faint smile, was taken by Alexander Gardner four days before the assassination. One print was made; the glass negative broke.

6. THE POWER
OF THE NORTH

ALL kinds of men—aristocrats and commoners, intellectuals and politicians, sensitive and insensitive observers—were convinced in 1861 that the North was heading into war under a leader who was pretty smalltime. Abraham Lincoln might be well intentioned, it was conceded, but he was no statesman. He did not look or act like one, and he certainly did not talk like one. Charles Francis Adams pronounced the cold verdict of upper-class New England: "Good-natured, kindly, honest, but frivolous and uncertain."

Other commentators were more brutal. In Washington gossip, in drawing-room conversations, in the press, Lincoln was referred to as a "baboon," an "ape" and a "mule." People talked about his social crudity, his lack of taste in language, and his weakness of character. Many never recovered from their first impressions. To the last they saw Lincoln as an amiable mediocrity, a loose administrator and a folksy failure—in short, as an incompetent and ineffective President. These were not only the judgments of Democrats, who might be expected to be hostile, but of members of Lincoln's own Republican party, of men who were his political intimates, of spokesmen for the antislavery groups. In fact, evaluations of Lincoln by his followers would constitute a formidable contribution to the literature of abuse.

"That sand-hill crane in the Presidential chair," exploded a New York newspaperman, ". . . the joking machine men call Abraham Lincoln." A Republican editor lamented in 1863: "He is an awful, woeful ass." In the same year

A PATRIOTIC POSTER, displayed after the outbreak of the Civil War, enjoins Northern loyalty. The flag, by Lincoln's direction, has no stars subtracted for the seceded states.

a leading Republican senator thus dismissed the President and his Cabinet: "The simple truth is, there never was such a shambling, half and half set of incapables collected in one government before since the world began. I saw a letter this morning written in good English by the King of Siam to Admiral Foote, which had more good sense in it, and a better comprehensiveness of our troubles . . . than *Abe* has had from the beginning."

Wendell Phillips, the eloquent orator of the antislavery movement, derided Lincoln in the most unmeasured terms: "We pay dear today for having as President a man so cautious as to be timid—and so ignorant as to fear the little near danger more than the danger farther off." He added: "As long as you keep the present turtle at the head of affairs, you make a pit with one hand and fill it with the other." There was something about this remarkable man that confused even those who knew him at close hand. He had greatness, but it eluded those who should have seen it first.

He was not easy to know. His law partner, William Herndon, said Lincoln was the most "shut-mouthed" man who ever lived. David Davis, who managed Lincoln's campaign in 1860, said: "He was the most reticent, secretive man I ever saw or expect to see." Although Davis had been very close to candidate Lincoln, President Lincoln never asked his advice on any question. It was Davis' impression that Lincoln asked nobody's advice and took none. "I asked him once about his cabinet. He said he never consulted his cabinet. He said they all disagreed so much, he would not ask them. He depended on himself always. . . . He said he ran the machine himself."

D AVIS' analysis pointed up a facet of Lincoln missed by most of his contemporaries and also by later critics. Lincoln was many things—a brooding mystic, a poet, a prophet, a folk symbol and a statesman of the highest order. But he was also a superb politician and a supreme power operator; in fact, one of the most consummate power artists in American history. Outwardly pliant and easygoing, he was inwardly as hard as iron, and when moving toward what he thought was a legitimate objective, he could be coldly ruthless. He was complex enough to realize the value of appearing simple. He was so confident of his own ability that he could afford to seem without power, or to let others seem to exercise power that was really his, or to accept seeming defeat if the result was what he wanted.

His habit of relating homely stories, which many dismissed as bantering humor, was in reality often a subtle exercise of power, and the stories generally pointed up some great truth. Once a group of Republican politicians descended on him to demand an active assignment for General John C. Frémont, who had not done well in the war and who had been relieved from duty. Lincoln said that he would like to oblige them but that he could not give Frémont a post without displacing some general already in command. The request reminded him, he went on, of the old man who kept urging his son to take a wife. The boy finally agreed but then asked: "Whose wife shall I take?" One of the delegation said that the appointment of Frémont would stir the country. Lincoln replied: "It would stir the country on one side, and stir it the other way on the other. It would please Frémont's friends, and displease the conservatives; and that is all I can see in the stirring argument."

On another occasion a Pennsylvania delegation called on him to demand a major general's appointment for Samuel P. Heintzelman, whom they de-

Charles Francis Adams, U.S. minister to England, could be a most outspoken diplomat. When Britain persisted in building ships for the South, Adams sent a note to the British foreign secretary in which he said bitingly: "It would be superfluous in me to point out to your lordship that this is war."

scribed as a deserving officer. Yes, agreed Lincoln, Heintzelman was "a good egg" and hence would keep; the Pennsylvanians would have to trust the President to do the right thing. After a tense pause, one of the visitors complained: "We have trusted you on this matter a long time." Rising to bow them out, Lincoln replied: "Gentlemen, you must do so longer."

With his great intelligence Lincoln was capable of outwitting almost any opponent he had to face. He ran the machine with such quiet art that few recognized the hand of the master. This man of the prairies embodied the national character: its virtues and defects, its practicality and its resolute determination. The same violent contrasts appeared in his person. Six foot four in height and weighing about 180 pounds, he was bony and angular and undeniably ugly. Yet there was an air of grandeur about him that some observers caught. An English visitor recorded an impression of eyes "that seemed to gaze through you without looking at you" and an aura of "strength, physical as well as moral, and a strange look of dignity."

Wendell Phillips, an impassioned abolitionist, had no cotton or cane sugar in his home because they were products of slave labor. He gave up law practice so he would not have to support a Constitution which permitted bondage. He even "seceded" from the Union in 1842, 19 years before the South did.

IN his choice of a Cabinet, Lincoln demonstrated immediately his confidence in his inner powers. He included in his official family four of the men who had been his rivals for the nomination, each of whom before 1860 was regarded as a bigger man than Lincoln. They were William H. Seward, Secretary of State; Salmon P. Chase, Secretary of the Treasury; Simon Cameron of Pennsylvania, Secretary of War; and Edward Bates of Missouri, Attorney General. It was, of course, good politics to appoint them. They brought unity to the Administration, and in the Cabinet they were always under Lincoln's eye. But they were potentially a difficult group to control, and Lincoln's choice indicated his belief in his managerial abilities.

The other members were Gideon Welles of Connecticut, Secretary of the Navy; Montgomery Blair of Maryland, Postmaster General; and Caleb Smith of Indiana, Secretary of the Interior. It was, on the whole, a strong Cabinet. Seward and Chase were definitely above average. The former, after a blundering beginning in which he seemed to think his mission was to restore American unity by provoking a European war, settled down to become an outstanding Secretary of State. Chase was no financial expert, but he had the mind to dominate his office and to make it an active force in the war effort.

Judge David Davis, Lincoln's campaign manager, was so fat it was said he had to be "surveyed" for a pair of trousers. Davis met Lincoln on the Illinois circuit and the young lawyer spoke of him as "my intimate friend." But Davis later observed wryly that Lincoln had been a man with no close friends.

Cameron, "the Czar of Pennsylvania," tall, lean, with a foxlike face, was above all else the professional politician. He had a reputation—which may or may not have been deserved—for sharp and even shady doings. His rival in the politics of the Keystone State, sarcastic Thaddeus Stevens, once told Lincoln he did not think Cameron would steal "a red-hot stove," the implication being that everything else had better be nailed down. The amused President repeated the remark to Cameron, who demanded an apology. Stevens came to Lincoln to retract: "I believe I told you he would not steal a red-hot stove. I will now take that back." Cameron proved to be a poor administrator and early in 1862 resigned his post at Lincoln's request. He was succeeded by Edwin M. Stanton, surly, rough and asthmatic, who brought energy and honesty to the direction of the War Department.

Bates, a sober, somewhat quaint individual, was a plodder, a good lawyer but no more. The bearded, bewigged Welles picked men with the right technical knowledge to advise him and proved to be a capable executive. "Uncle Gideon," as Lincoln called him, was unswervingly loyal to the President, as

A is America,

land of the free.

B is a Battle,

our soldiers did see.

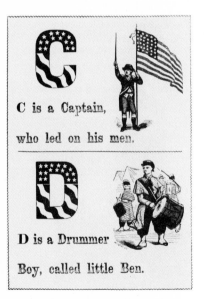

C is a Captain,

who led on his men.

D is a Drummer

Boy, called little Ben.

During the Civil War, Northern children learned their ABCs from this patriotic primer, illustrated with soldiers and battle scenes. In his enthusiasm the artist even included a Revolutionary War captain—with a 34-star flag. The war caused an upheaval in the South's schools: Northern texts had been used almost exclusively but after 1861 the South hastily wrote its own.

was the bald, cadaverous Blair in his less important post. Smith was a political appointee to a department that then was the least in the Cabinet.

Not unnaturally, Seward thought he should be the man in the head job. The fortunes of politics had ordained otherwise, but the smart little New Yorker confidently expected to act as "prime minister," to guide the inexperienced man from the prairies. Right at the outset Seward made his play for power. He presented to Lincoln a curious paper titled "Some Thoughts for the President's Consideration." It said, in effect, that the government was drifting without a policy, that it ought to have a policy and that William H. Seward would be happy to frame one and administer it.

The patronizing tone might well have infuriated Lincoln, but he met the challenge perfectly. In his reply he said that he was always glad to receive advice from his official family, but that he alone was President and he alone would determine policy. Seward promptly subsided and from that moment became Lincoln's loyal subordinate. The two men were much together during the war years. They liked each other's company. Both were good storytellers, and their temperaments were similar: genial, conservative and tolerant.

Seward yielded because he grasped that Lincoln was a bigger man than he was. This truth could never have occurred to the Secretary of the Treasury; no man, and least of all the raw Lincoln, could possibly be bigger than Salmon P. Chase. Tall, portly, handsome, with a head that has been compared to Webster's, Chase thought he was as impressive as he looked. His is one of the strangest cases in the annals of American politics. Able and principled, he was still curiously unattractive, with an unnatural arrogance and pomposity about him. "He thinks there is a fourth person in the Trinity," said one of his critics. Most unnatural of all was his ambition to be President. He wanted it so badly that he demeaned himself to get it. He never realized that he had stooped, because his ambition was not narrowly personal. The presidency deserved him—and he was merely trying to give the country the best.

While he was a member of the Cabinet, Chase made a move to get the 1864 Republican presidential nomination and saw nothing improper in the effort. His candidacy collapsed rather ignominiously, and afterward he found an occasion to resign. He had threatened resignation many times before, but always Lincoln had said he could not do without him. This time the President accepted the offer, to Chase's surprise. Lincoln had put up with Chase's pretensions while he could use him for the good of the country and the war. He dispensed with the secretary when his usefulness was ended, supplanting him with William Pitt Fessenden of Maine. But later, on the death of Chief Justice Taney, Lincoln named Chase to preside over the Supreme Court.

LINCOLN possessed in ample quantity the attributes of a great war leader. He had infinite patience, iron resolution, high intelligence and a power to employ language that fired men's souls. As an administrator he was technically deficient, being careless of detail and routine. But his position did not demand a good desk man. He had to unite his people to fight for an abstract ideal—the Union—and to nerve them to continue the struggle through years of bitter and bloody frustration. His concept of the sacredness of the American experiment in government was almost mystic, and he would do anything to preserve it.

He would, notably, mobilize the full authority of his office, the great war powers of the President, behind the war for the Union. As Commander in Chief he announced by proclamation a state of insurrection or, really, of war; again by proclamation invoked a naval blockade of the South, and increased the size of the military forces in defiance of the Constitution. Also without legal sanction, he authorized the expenditure of money that had never been appropriated by Congress. He would be recreant to his oath of office, he felt, if he was afraid to disregard sections of the Constitution to save the government; he would not lose the whole by being too tender about violating a part. In cases where the fundamental document did not clearly state whether it was the President or Congress who should exercise certain powers, Lincoln boldly assumed that the President should act.

One of his techniques was to confront Congress with an accomplished deed and ask the helpless legislators to ratify it. Lincoln and other Northern leaders often demonstrated a true revolutionary zeal; they did what they had to do to get results. Supposedly the North represented law and the South revolution. But in the making of war, the men of the North were revolutionists, the men of the South legalists. Both sides were reflecting a principle of their system—the North looked to the moving future, the South to the static past.

Clad only in underwear, Clement Vallandigham (above) is arrested by Union soldiers who broke into his home at night. The leader of the dissenting Copperheads—who are depicted below as a snake hissing at the fair maiden Union—was ordered taken after he declared the North was waging the Civil War "for the freedom of the blacks and the enslavement of the whites."

THE most striking and continuous employment of a presidential war power by Lincoln was his suspension of the writ of habeas corpus to suppress opposition to the military effort. Opposition to the war centered in two groups —Southern sympathizers in the loyal slave states, and the faction of the Democratic party known as the Peace Democrats, or Copperheads. Of the two, the latter were more important, and Lincoln's action against them aroused wide criticism. The Southern sympathizers, operating in areas that were actual or potential battle theaters, were obvious enemies. But it was not so easy to classify Copperheads as disloyal.

Three factions were present in the wartime Democratic party. One was a minority, the War Democrats, who were willing to support the war to the extent of taking offices under the Administration. The mass of the Democrats rendered general support to the war program but freely and sometimes intemperately attacked specific actions of the Administration.

The third faction, the Peace Democrats, was also a minority, but it commanded a strong following in the Western states. Indeed, these Western Democrats exhibited a sectionalism almost as pronounced as that of Southern Democrats. They believed that the industrial East had for years exploited the farming regions and that its instrument of control was federal power. In their devotion to agrarian ideals and states' rights they were curiously like Southerners. Their chief spokesman, Ohio's Clement L. Vallandigham, tall, handsome and humorless, a kind of Western Sumner, once declared: "I am as good a Western fire-eater as the hottest salamander in this House." And again: "I . . . am wholly devoted to Western interests. . . . I became and am a *Western sectionalist,* and so shall continue to the day of my death."

Passionately convinced that the war was evil in intent, the Peace Democrats proposed a simple way to end it: make an armistice and withdraw the armies from the field. Then, after a brief healing period the South would voluntarily return to the fold and a national convention could be called to amend the Constitution to guarantee states' rights. It did not occur to them that the South would not go along with this quixotic program, that it would regard an armistice as a recognition of the Confederacy's independence.

Most Copperheads were Unionists, although in a strange and impractical way, but some advocated the formation of a third, a Western, confederacy. Some created secret societies with such intriguing names as Knights of the Golden Circle, which allegedly aimed to aid the Confederacy by stirring up rebellion in the North. The government was never able to document precisely its charges against the societies, but no documentation was needed to establish the public policy of the Copperheads. In speeches and newspaper editorials they denounced the war as an unjust conflict that had to be stopped. Vallandigham charged that the purpose of the Administration in waging the war was to convert the present democratic system into "an imperial despotism." He added: "I did not support the war; and today I bless God that not the smell of so much as one drop of its blood is upon my garments." An Iowa Copperhead said shrilly: "With all his vast armies Lincoln has failed, *failed*, FAILED, FAILED! And still the monster usurper wants more victims for his slaughter pens. . . . His cry is ever for more blood."

Against both Copperheads and Southern supporters Lincoln used the weapon of military arrests. By suspending the right of habeas corpus, which normally prevents unlawful detention of a citizen, the government could apprehend opponents of the war and hold them indefinitely without trial or bring them to trial before military courts. The Constitution stated clearly that habeas corpus could be suspended but did not say who was to do the suspending. Lincoln assumed, as he did in other areas, that the President was the only agent who could act effectively, and he suspended the writ in specified areas and for specified times. In 1863 Congress, not very willingly, authorized him to resort to martial law, and he then announced a general suspension.

At least 13,000 persons and possibly thousands more were arrested during the war years. The great majority were ordinary people, but a few were prominent individuals, including several members of the Maryland legislature and Vallandigham, the top Copperhead. Nothing like it had been seen since the Revolution—and the events of that era had been largely local affairs. In the conflicts since then, opposition had been accepted as normal, as something that could be safely tolerated. But this war was different. It was a big, lethal, modern struggle of unlimited objectives, the forerunner of the total wars. In those later conflicts the unity that Lincoln reluctantly sought to enforce by martial law would be imposed by the will of society itself.

As if the Democrats were not enough, Lincoln faced factionalism and opposition in his own party. This division was not over what the government's objectives should be, but over the method and timing to be employed in reaching them. The Republicans were in most areas of action a remarkably united party; in a general way they knew their economic and political goals and moved methodically toward them. But on one issue they divided, and this issue overshadowed all others. It was slavery or, specifically, the wartime disposition to be made of slavery. On this question the Republicans divided into factions, calling themselves Radicals and Conservatives.

The Radicals were represented by men like Charles Sumner and Ben Wade of the Senate and crusty old Thaddeus Stevens in the House. They were true radicals, as they proudly acknowledged, in that they wanted to accomplish a sweeping social change immediately. Opposed to slavery in an intense and

Lincoln is shown preparing to issue his Emancipation Proclamation in a Northern engraving (above) and Southern cartoon (below). Although Lincoln was not an abolitionist, he was strongly opposed to slavery. On signing the proclamation he remarked to Secretary of State Seward: "If my name ever goes into history, it will be for this act, and my whole soul is in it."

even doctrinaire way, they wanted to use the opportunity of the war to strike the institution down. The Conservatives were a smaller and less sharply marked group. Although they differed on details, they all desired some gradual and delayed form of emancipation, to take place after the war.

Both factions, then, were for the Union, and both were antislavery. But one would add the abolition of slavery to the aim of preserving the nation, while the other would save the Union without experimenting with social change beyond what seemed absolutely necessary. Lincoln was generally regarded as a Conservative, and the label was on the whole accurate. He favored a gradual approach to emancipation, and he was acutely aware of the problems for both races that would follow a sudden alteration in relations. Still he was not so conservative that he would refuse to take any action at all. He sympathized with the Radical objective and was willing to move toward it—if the move would not endanger his larger objective of saving the Union.

THE logic of events pushed the North inexorably along the road to emancipation. At the beginning of the war, public opinion favored fighting for only one aim: restoring the Union. Congress made this the nation's official objective by approving a resolution which stated that the war was not being waged for the purpose of interfering with the domestic institutions of any state. But such a view could prevail only in a short war. The Northern people were not going to sacrifice for any long period while preserving an institution that in common opinion was responsible for the war. Within little more than a year after the opening guns, Northern patience began to wear thin.

In July of 1862 the Radicals were able to push through Congress a bold endeavor to force emancipation by legislative action. This Confiscation Act declared the property of persons supporting the insurrection subject to seizure by the federal government (but because of the threat of a Lincoln veto, the forfeiture was not valid beyond the natural life of the offender); it proclaimed free the slaves of persons aiding and abetting the insurrection, and it authorized the President to employ blacks, including freed slaves, in the military service. It was and remained a paper edict without much practical effect. The property of rebels could not be confiscated without going through a cumbersome judicial process, and in any event the act could have no force until the South was occupied. But it was a sign of a vital shift in mass opinion, and the effect was not lost on the master politician in the White House.

Lincoln was a supreme combination of principle and pragmatism. Profoundly antislavery, he did not think that he had any right because of his official position to enforce his private convictions by striking at the institution. Nor would he jeopardize his larger policy of saving the Union for the gratification of weakening slavery. He would not, in short, make even a right change at the wrong time, before there was a need for it or before public opinion was ready for it. But the events of the summer of 1862 convinced him that the moment for change had arrived. If the Northern people wanted slavery destroyed, he could not and would not oppose their desire.

The Radicals were riding high, and unless Lincoln put himself at the head of the antislavery movement they might run away with it. In that July when the Confiscation Act was passed, Lincoln decided to issue an executive proclamation, based on his war powers, freeing slaves in the Confederacy as a military measure. He informed his Cabinet that he had prepared a draft of

In an anti-Union British cartoon of 1862, an upside-down Lincoln swings perilously from one hanging ring to another as European royalty and the cheering common folk look on. He has successfully traversed "Buncomb" (or "bunkum"), "Brag" and "Paper Money." Now, muscles taut, face straining, he proceeds from "Emancipation" to the final ring: "Utter Ruin."

such a proclamation. Seward advised that its issuance be withheld until after a military success, lest it seem that the government was uttering a "last shriek on the retreat." Lincoln considered the suggestion good and put the document aside. But no victories came, only sickening defeats.

At last in September a Confederate offensive was turned back at the battle of Antietam in Maryland. On the 22nd, Lincoln opened a Cabinet meeting by reading a selection from the latest book of the popular humorist Artemus Ward, who specialized in rural dialect. Then shifting to a graver mood, the President read a draft of what he called his preliminary proclamation. It warned the areas in rebellion that unless they returned to their allegiance by January 1, 1863, he would issue a final proclamation declaring their slaves free. The Cabinet approved the draft, with some minor revisions, and two days later it was given to the world.

No state came back, and on the first day of the new year Lincoln issued the famous document known as the Emancipation Proclamation. He signed it after shaking hands with thousands of people at the traditional White House New Year's reception. When the sheet was spread before him he remarked: "I never in my life felt more certain that I was doing right than I do in signing this paper. But I have been receiving calls and shaking hands since nine o'clock this morning, till my arm is stiff and numb. Now this signature is one that will be closely examined, and if they find my hand trembled they will say, 'He had some compunctions.' But anyway, it is going to be done." He took the pen and wrote at the bottom, not the customary "A. Lincoln," but in bold characters "Abraham Lincoln."

THE proclamation declared forever free the slaves in the rebellious states. But not all areas in the Confederacy were included within the scope of the document. Excepted was the whole state of Tennessee, also the southern part of Louisiana and the western part of Virginia. They were the only sections of the Confederacy then occupied by Union troops and the only ones therefore where the proclamation could have any immediate effect. Presumably they were excluded because they were not enemy territory and hence not subject to the President's war powers.

The proclamation had other limitations. It could not apply to the loyal slave states. It did not immediately free any slaves in the Confederate states and would not free any until Union armies occupied the South. Nor did it affect the legal basis of slavery, which as an institution could be abolished only by individual state action or an amendment to the Constitution. Still the issuance of the proclamation was a momentous event. Eventually thousands and thousands of slaves were set free by its terms. Most important, it signified that the war had taken a new turn. It was to be a war for freedom now as well as Union, and from this position there could be no retreat.

As Lincoln said, revolutions never go backward but proceed relentlessly to their end. The only end there could be after 1863 was complete abolition. Shortly after the war, the 13th Amendment was ratified. It freed all slaves in the land and destroyed slavery as an institution. The Northern people in 1861 had had no intention of changing the status of slavery. But great wars make their own conditions. So it was with the Civil War. That war swept up the whole nation and impelled it along a course it never dreamed it would follow.

In 1864 Lincoln and his Administration, now committed to the double war

Poking fun at Lincoln's liking for jokes, this 1864 Democratic cartoon shows presidential candidate George McClellan delivering part of Hamlet's soliloquy ("Where be your jibes now?") to Lincoln's head. The real McClellan (below) repeatedly revealed his contempt for the Commander in Chief. He once referred to Lincoln as "nothing more than a well-meaning baboon."

aims of Union and emancipation, had to submit their chances to the voters in a presidential election. Many Republicans, still looking on Lincoln as a small man, preferred another candidate, and the Radicals in particular stood against him because he had not done things their way. "I hope we may not be compelled to push him four years more," wrote young Congressman James A. Garfield. It was a typical reaction. A friend of Lincoln's canvassed both houses of Congress and reported to the President that he could find hardly a member who favored his renomination. A Pennsylvania visitor asked Thaddeus Stevens to introduce him to some congressmen who supported Lincoln. "Old Thad" took him to Isaac N. Arnold, from a Chicago district, and said: "Here is a man who wants to find a Lincoln member of Congress. You are the only one I know, and I have come over to introduce my friend to you."

But no rival candidate appeared who was able to develop a real challenge. Lincoln may have been unpopular with the politicians, but he was popular with the people. When the party—technically known that year as the Union party—held its convention in June it nominated Lincoln, although with no great enthusiasm, and to balance the ticket it awarded the vice-presidential post to Andrew Johnson of Tennessee, a War Democrat who had refused to go along with his seceding state.

The Democratic Convention was not scheduled to meet until August, and as the hot weeks of summer wore on, the signs seemed to portend a Republican defeat. War weariness had settled on much of the North. The conflict was well into its fourth year, and victory seemed as distant as ever. Actually, the military crisis had been passed in the previous year, and the South had no chance whatever to win a military decision if the North only kept on fighting. But to many people the cause appeared hopeless and their frustration was translated into a revulsion against the party running the war.

Lincoln himself was fully prepared for political defeat. One day he sat in his study and drew up an interesting paper. Later he asked his Cabinet members to sign it, without showing them the contents. It stated that probably the Administration would not be re-elected and that it was the duty of every signer to cooperate with the Democratic President-elect between November and March to save the Union "as he will have secured his election on such ground that he can not possibly save it afterwards." Some of the Radical leaders hopefully observed Lincoln's fading chances and hatched a scheme to force him off the ticket and put one of their own in his place.

T HEN suddenly a dramatic reversal of fortunes occurred. The Democrats met and nominated a man hated by Republicans, George B. McClellan, who as a general had opposed the Radical emancipation program. And the Peace faction got a plank in the platform denouncing the war as a failure and calling for an armistice to be followed by a convention of all the states. As the armistice would be invoked without requiring the South to agree to come to the convention, the Democrats, whether they realized it or not, were paving the way for Confederate independence. McClellan finally repudiated the peace plank, but officially the Democrats stood forth as the peace party.

The Democratic Convention put a new face on the matter for all Republicans and most of all for the Radicals. As bad as Lincoln was in their eyes, he was infinitely better than McClellan on a peace platform. Grimly the Republicans prepared to close ranks. Then the military situation shifted abruptly

"Long Abraham a Little Longer" is the title of this cartoon which appeared in "Harper's" just after Lincoln's re-election. During the campaign Lincoln said: "Supporting General McClellan . . . is no violation of army regulations, and as a question of taste of choosing between him and me, well, I'm the longest, but he's better looking." Soldiers chose Lincoln, three to one.

119

to favor Lincoln. A series of victories, including the capture in September of the Confederate base of Atlanta, raised popular hopes again and practically guaranteed Republican success. In the November election Lincoln rolled up an impressive electoral triumph, 212 votes to McClellan's 21. But his popular margin was only 400,000 votes out of a total of four million. Still the American people had returned a tough answer to a tough choice. They had been asked to decide between the easy way of peace and the hard way of war—and they had rejected the soft solution.

THE one area of war leadership in which Lincoln had the least competence was economics. He knew his deficiency and largely left the problems of financing the war effort to Secretary Chase. But he did grasp the significance of the war for the American economy, and in some of his most eloquent expressions he emphasized that the American nation was so inherently strong that it could simultaneously fight a great war and expand its material wealth.

The wartime expansion was something to arouse pride. In part, it was simply a continuation of a process begun before the war. Some industries actually were retarded by the war, suffering from shortages of supplies or labor, but industry as a whole and agriculture, responding to the stimulus of governmental demands, boosted production to previously undreamed of totals. The output of coal jumped from 19 million tons in 1861 to over 24 million in 1864. On the eve of the war the principal government arsenals were manufacturing only 22,000 rifles a year, but in 1862 the Springfield plant alone turned out 200,000. In 1861 shipments of iron ore on the Great Lakes totaled 45,000 tons; in 1863 ships carried 235,000 tons to the greedy mills of Pittsburgh. The freight tonnage carried on the railroads soared to fantastic new highs, increasing on some lines by as much as 100 per cent. Agricultural production shot up comparably. The average annual wheat exports during the war were over four times greater than in the prewar decade. Wool production in the North climbed from 48 million pounds in 1860 to 97 million pounds in 1864.

Production in all fields was augmented by enlarging existing facilities or constructing new ones. In one year, as an example, 57 new factories rose in Philadelphia. But increased production was accomplished most significantly by employing devices or processes known before the war but not widely utilized until the devouring demands of war took over. Machines which did the work of many human hands enabled industry to increase its production while

The "greenback," first U.S. paper money, sported a portrait of Salmon Chase, the Secretary of the Treasury. On the back were the now-familiar words: "This note is a legal tender" (above). As gold and silver coins became increasingly scarce, someone wrote an ode to "the last silver dollar, / Left shining alone, / All its laughing companions / Have melted and gone."

using fewer laborers, and more than made up for the loss of thousands of the worker force to the armies. The Howe-Singer sewing machine in textiles and the McKay shoe stitcher revolutionized their industries; in agriculture the McCormick reaper made permanent changes in methods of wheat culture. Driven by the fierce energy of war, the American economy took a giant step toward mass production.

The economy received another potent stimulant from the wartime legislation enacted by the Republican Congress. The Republicans were committed to the philosophy that government had a role to play in economic growth, that it should encourage private enterprise with direct aid and subsidies. With Southern opposition removed, the Republican majority proceeded to put its ideals into practice and to redeem its platform pledges of 1860 to the Northern economic combinations that had placed it in power.

The Homestead Act made it possible for a settler to acquire without payment a farm of 160 acres in the public domain. The Morrill Land Grant Act gratified another Western demand by donating to the states land to be used for the purpose of establishing agricultural colleges. Tariff protection for domestic industry reached an unprecedented level. Provision was at last made for the transcontinental railroad through Nebraska by chartering two national corporations, the Union Pacific and the Central Pacific, which were to receive generous financial assistance. The National Bank Act restored the connection between the government and the banking community which had been destroyed 30 years before by the Jacksonian Democrats. The National Banks received their charters from the national government, they were required to purchase stipulated amounts of government bonds, and with the bonds as a basis they could issue bank notes that circulated as currency.

Doing their part, women manufacture cartridges for Union muskets at the arsenal in Watertown, Massachusetts. The work was dangerous and in 1864 an explosion killed 18 girls. Lincoln once told a soldier that "all that has been said by orators and poets since the creation of the world in praise of women . . . would not do them justice for their conduct during the war."

WITH its vast stores of wealth, the North should have been able to support the war effort with no particular strain. But the government approached its financial problems in a hesitant spirit and failed to exploit adequately the available sources of income. Its failure was the result not of stupidity on the part of Chase or the congressional leaders but of national inexperience.

For a people who had not paid any direct taxes since 1817, a war that eventually cost two million dollars a day was almost incomprehensible. Secretary Chase feared the effect of high taxes on public opinion and hoped to finance the war largely by borrowing. Not until 1862 did Congress bring itself to pass an internal revenue act that reached, although with low rates, practically all goods and occupations. The Treasury's income from bonds was four times as much as from all other sources combined. To provide money, Congress authorized the issuance of a special paper currency, known as "greenbacks."

The greenbacks were a practical necessity, but being unredeemable in specie they inflated prices and contributed to increasing the government's own costs. They and the national bank notes were, however, a part of a vitally important historical process. For the first time America had a national currency. It also had, and for the first time, a national tax system, a national bank system, national aid for education and national financing of great transportation projects. Nobody had planned it that way. But as a result of the Civil War the concept of states' rights and localism was going down everywhere. It was giving way in the North just as surely as its political expression in the South would be destroyed by the war.

WAVING FLAGS and beating a drum recruiters seeking volunteers for the "Bucktail" regiment draw a crowd of fired-up Philadelphians. Despite the warning on their band wagon, conscription did not begin in the North until after two years of war.

A people rallying to Old Glory

IT seems as if we never were alive till now; never had a country till now." So wrote a New York girl of the patriotic excitement touched off in the North by the attack on Fort Sumter. To the sound of ringing bells and wild huzzahs, Lincoln's message calling for 75,000 volunteers was read aloud on village greens and in city squares. Armories were jammed with recruits. On April 19, 1861, only a few days after Sumter fell, the first New York regiment was ready to depart. Wearing uniforms from Brooks Brothers and carrying sandwiches from Delmonico's, the troops swung down Broadway with jubilant crowds cheering them off to Washington, D.C. "It was worth a life, that march," exulted one soldier. Like many another, he would soon pay that price in battle.

Cries of solidarity rang out from every part of the Union. "The West," came a report, "is all one great Eagle-scream!" A Massachusetts soldier, asked how many from his state were joining up, replied laconically, "All of us." A Philadelphian declared, "There is among us but one thought, one object, one end, one symbol—the Stars and Stripes." Few people could see beyond the monster rallies and their own optimism to the long bloody conflict that lay ahead. But as the massive mobilization of the North gained momentum, one Confederate observer said soberly: "What we have to do must be done quickly. The longer we have them to fight the more difficult they will be to defeat."

IN PATRIOTIC FAREWELL, an officer's beloved consecrates his sword to the Union cause. Some women, less demure but more spirited, shamed their menfolk into joining up.

UNION FOR EVER

O. K. HOUSE

DINING SALOON FREE FOR VOLUNTEER

HOT COFFEE AND REFRESHMENT FREE FOR THE UNION VOLUNTEERS

WATER   WATER   WATER   WATER

PHILADELPHIA & BALTIMOR

WASHING DEPARTMENT

INTERIOR OF DINING SALOON FREE FOR UNION VOLUNTEERS

Entered according to Act of Congress in the Year 1861 by B.S. Brown, in the clerks office of the District Court of the Southern District of Pennsylvania

PUB BY B. S. BROWN. 110 SOUTH ST. PHIL.

VOLUNTEER REFRESHMENT SALOON, SUPPORTED GRATUITOUSLY BY TH

Legions of ladies at work on the home front

WOMEN of the North rallied to their cause in countless ways. They knitted and sewed, served food to troops in transit *(left)*, replaced men as workers in offices and factories, and labored diligently to feed and clothe the needy families of Union volunteers.

Thousands of women's aid societies were formed. Although in the South these aid agencies remained loosely organized, in the North their efforts were coordinated by the Sanitary Commission, set up in June 1861 to care for sick and wounded soldiers. By raising funds in "sanitary fairs" *(below)*, the Northern ladies helped bring better hygiene to camps and hospitals—thus combating the diseases that swept the armies all through the war.

A FAIR IN BROOKLYN, one of the many staged to raise war-relief funds, holds a vast sale of donated articles *(above)*. All its events, including a ball and quilting bee, netted $400,000.

A CANTEEN IN PHILADELPHIA welcomes battlebound units *(top)* and dispenses free meals *(interior, below)*. By January 1862 its staff of volunteers had served some 100,000 soldiers.

Ingenious measures to raise and uniform the troops

ON the eve of war, the U.S., traditionally wary of a strong standing army, had only 15,000 troops. By July 1861, the divided nation boasted forces of almost 300,000. Six months later, 575,000 men were under arms in the North alone, plus 350,000 more in the South.

Even these figures fell short of enlistment goals, but they represented a great triumph over inexperience and inefficiency. The states on both sides were permitted to raise troops as they saw fit. In practice, most units were recruited by local citizens eager to be elected officers. Once a company had been filled, it was enrolled in the state militia and equipped haphazardly, often by community donation or by the officers themselves. Many a man, shopping around to enlist, found little to choose between companies but their uniforms, and these were tailored in gaudy profusion to catch his eye. As more and more men doffed their mufti, outfits as exotic as the Zouaves' became commonplace—not just in the big cities (above), but also in small towns that had seen their first soldier less than a year before.

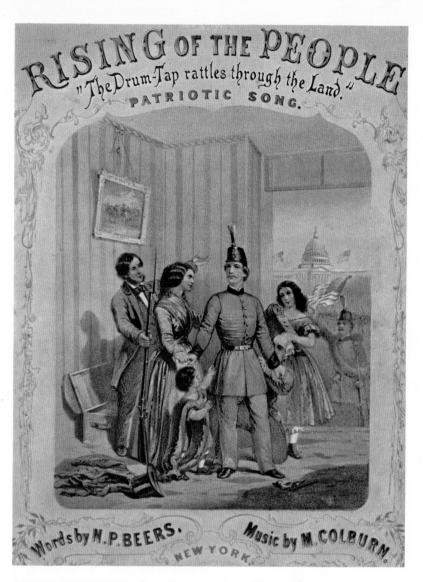

A SENTIMENTAL PRINT adorns the cover of a militant song, offered for sale at 50 cents. Many lyrics leavened the theme of patriotism with lavish praise for "the girl I left behind me."

A SPRINKLING OF UNIFORMS brightens a wartime gathering *(above)* in a New York bar. The Zouave *(foreground)* wears baggy pants and fez adapted from an Algerian original. The kilted man at the bar may have been a visitor; New York had a kilted regiment but it wore a different tartan.

A TRAIN OF SOLDIERS is cheered onward *(right)* to battle. At every way-stop the troops were "serenaded by brass bands, presented with silk flags, and inundated with speeches and prayers"—receptions which one skeptic said were "well calculated to stiffen their resolution to fight."

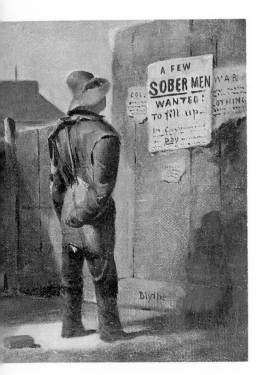

A TELLTALE POSTER, calling for "a few sober men," reflects the decline in volunteers after the first flush of war fever. Soon the North offered bounties to stimulate enlistment.

A last parade on the threshold of battle

Although Union men hurried to enlist and were rushed to Washington, forces to defend the city were so slow getting there that Lincoln exclaimed, "I don't believe there is any North!" But after three months enough regiments were amassed to stage a stirring parade down Pennsylvania Avenue *(right)*. Then they crossed the Potomac for their maiden battle, First Bull Run.

After that clash, hopes for a short and glorious war began fading in both armies. "I had a dim notion about the 'romance' of a soldier's life, etc.," one volunteer grimly confessed. *"I have got bravely over it since."*

7. THE PLIGHT OF THE SOUTH

O͏N a spring evening late in his life, Jefferson Davis sat with his wife and daughter on the veranda of Beauvoir, their home on the Mississippi Gulf Coast. Suddenly the daughter turned to the old man and asked what he would like best to be if he had his life to live over. She could see his eyes shine in the gloaming as he answered without hesitation: "I would be a cavalry officer and break squares." The remark was tragically revealing. It was not just that the onetime President of the Confederate States would rather have had a military career than the civilian role that history had cast him in. It was the absence of realism in the fine words. At any time when he could have been a cavalry leader, the forces of technology had invested "squares" of infantry formations with such firepower that horse charges on them would be suicidal. Davis did not understand this even in his presumably wise old age. There were many things about the modern world that Davis did not understand. It was his tragedy and the tragedy of the people he led in war so gallantly that both were in large part alien to that world against which they had rebelled and whose course they thought they could arrest.

An English reporter saw the Confederate President in 1861 at his capital in the little Alabama town of Montgomery. He noted the "slight, light figure, little exceeding middle height"; the head "well formed, with a fine full forehead, square and high . . . features regular, the cheekbones are too high, and the jaws too hollow to be handsome"; the lips "thin, flexible, and curved . . .

REBEL PRESIDENT Jefferson Davis, somber in this portrait by John Robertson, reflects the painful ailments and the weighty cares of office that wracked his frail physique.

131

and the eyes deep-set, large and full—one seems nearly blind, and is partly covered with a film, owing to excruciating attacks of neuralgia and tic"; the expression on the face "anxious . . . haggard, careworn, and pain-drawn."

The description caught well the outer Davis and hinted at some of his inner tensions. The strains he lived with were partly inherent in his personality make-up and partly the product of his Southern culture. Davis was a first-generation aristocrat. His family, coming out of ordinary economic circumstances, had amassed great wealth suddenly in the lush cotton lands of the Mississippi delta. Most of the civil leaders of the Confederacy were of this newly rich caste; hardly one could trace a distinguished ancestry back to the colonial period. They were new men, but they all rendered homage to the ideals of the Old South and cast themselves in its plantation image.

At Alabama's state house in Montgomery, Jefferson Davis is inaugurated provisional President of the Confederacy in "the grandest pageant ever witnessed in the South." But the travel difficulties the leaders braved to reach Montgomery boded ill for the waging of war. Davis had to journey 600 miles by rail, though his plantation (opposite) was only 285 miles away.

DAVIS was an outstanding representative of the ruling class of the cotton South, and it was because of his reputation and record—senator from Mississippi, Secretary of War under Pierce, able advocate of the Southern cause in debate—that he had been chosen President. He was selected too because he was known as a firm but not extreme secessionist. The government makers at Montgomery had been pathetically eager to demonstrate to their people and to the world that their nation was not radical but conservative. They had passed over the extremists like Yancey for the quieter Davis, and to conciliate those who had been reluctant to secede, they had elected as Vice President a moderate, Alexander H. Stephens of Georgia.

Davis possessed many fine abilities, but most of them were not the qualities that make a war leader great. He had an above-average mind, strong and logical. But his mind was part of his undoing. He was too proud of it, too sensitive about the correctness of his opinions, too sure that he was always right. In letters he carried on long disputes with generals and politicians in which his objective was to win a theoretical victory, to prove that he was right and they wrong. He really thought that they would be gratified to see their errors pointed out. His intellectualism dominated his language. His state papers and public addresses were admirable exercises in logic, but they were cold and unmoving. Davis could reach men's minds but not their hearts.

He tried to employ patience and tact in dealing with people, and up to a point he succeeded. But nearly always his control snapped, and he was capable of hurt fury and unreasoning obstinacy. He once admitted: "I have an infirmity of which I am heartily ashamed: when I am aroused in a matter, I lose control of my feelings and become personal." In part his reactions rose out of his own nature—his undue sensitivity to criticism and his precarious health and uncertain nerves. They were also the result of his culture. Davis and other Southern leaders were of a ruling class, accustomed to dealing with subordinates but not with equals. They were proud, taut, touchy and easily offended. Nor were they accustomed to the discipline of dull, routine work; when subjected to it they frayed under the strain and broke out at each other.

On the face of it Davis should have been a better war director than Lincoln. He was a graduate of West Point; he had had experience as an officer in the regular army and battle experience as a volunteer in the Mexican War. And he had been Secretary of War. But again an apparent merit turned into a defect. Davis' military background, coupled with his conviction of his superior intelligence, convinced him that he was more of an expert than he was. He could never forget that he had been a soldier and that at Buena Vista in Mexico he had led a wedge formation that won the field—a favorite saying of wartime wags was that the Confederacy was dying of an inverted V—and he would have preferred to be a general above all else. He not only exercised a close supervision over the military machine, which would have been perfectly proper in the largest sense, but he wasted his time on matters that should have been left to subordinates. An official in the War Department recorded that once there were 1,500 papers, all touching on appointments, on the desk of the Secretary of War. The secretary could not pass on them until the President looked at them, which would take him a week if he did nothing else. Davis, exclaimed the disgusted functionary, was absorbed in "little trash."

Technically he was a fine administrator, much better than Lincoln, but his role did not call for efficient attention to paper work. His devotion to form was a reflection of both his personality and his society. Southerners were conservative and legal-minded people. They had set up an organization that they called a nation, and having gone through the ritual they thought they had a nation. Davis and other Southern leaders assumed that the Confederacy could act as a going nation and fight a formal war, whereas the situation called for radical and even revolutionary action.

Lincoln, at the head of a stronger government, ruthlessly grasped the power to suspend habeas corpus. But Davis, proceeding legally, asked his Congress for permission to suspend and received a limited authorization. Davis and other Confederates cannot be fairly criticized for not acting like revolutionaries. Restricted by their culture, they could not have done other than they did. But the restriction constituted a tragic limitation, especially in a modern war against a modern government. "All the revolutionary vigor is with the enemy," complained one Confederate observer who saw the fatal drift of events.

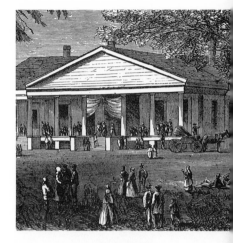

In this pair of fine homes Jefferson Davis lived a frustrating life. To support his family, he gave up his precious army career and became a planter; his home after 1852 was Brierfield (above) in Mississippi. Later, as Confederate President, he resided in the Brockenbrough house (below) in Richmond, though he would have much preferred to be off in battle commanding troops.

WHEN Davis selected his Cabinet, he assumed that every state except his own Mississippi should be represented by a seat. His reasoning was sound enough—a body so chosen would presumably unite public opinion—but the result was that some men were named to posts for which they were not fitted because posts they could fill had to go to men from other states. For example, Georgia's Robert Toombs, a rough, blunt character, became Secretary of State. He was knowledgeable in finance and should have had the Treasury portfolio. But South Carolina had to have something, and the only available individual from that state whom Davis was willing to appoint was Christopher G. Memminger, a Charleston lawyer who was supposed to understand monetary problems. So the stern and humorless Memminger, an honest but uninspired plodder, went in as Secretary of the Treasury.

The Secretary of War was Leroy Pope Walker, a tall, angular, tobacco-chewing Alabama lawyer. Walker was a poor administrator who could not even keep up with his correspondence. "That slow coach," the acid diarist Mrs. Chesnut called him, and she added that if a Napoleon showed up in the South the secretary would refuse him a commission. Walker soon found an occasion to resign. Heading the Navy Department was Florida's Stephen R. Mallory, rotund and ruddy, who as a senator in the old Union had specialized in naval affairs. He turned out to be an exceptionally competent administrator, as did the unpretentious John H. Reagan of Texas, who was Postmaster General. Judah P. Benjamin of Louisiana, the ablest individual in the group,

was named to the comparatively unimportant position of Attorney General.

It was a Cabinet of shifting personnel. Of the original appointees, only Mallory and Reagan served throughout the war. There were three Secretaries of State, two Secretaries of the Treasury, five Secretaries of War and four Attorneys General. Benjamin showed up in two additional posts after starting out as Attorney General—War and State—and he held the latter office longer than any other incumbent. "There was no circle, official or otherwise, that missed his soft, purring presence," said one critic. On the whole it was not a strong Cabinet; the level of ability reached at best only competency. Mallory and Reagan were good directors of their departments, as were Virginians George W. Randolph and James A. Seddon, two of the several war secretaries; but no one of them showed much imagination or independence.

Benjamin possibly possessed some of the elements of greatness. But either because he did not own strong convictions or because he felt it was futile to try to influence Davis, he did not seek to impose his will outside his department. He ran whichever office he held well, but his really fine mind never counted as a force in determining policy. Benjamin and the other members of the first Cabinet embodied the social system of the cotton South. Except for Toombs and Walker, who could point to lineages of some prestige, it was a collection of men who had come up out of ordinary and in some cases obscure beginnings. Three were foreign-born first-generation Americans. Memminger had been born in Germany and had spent part of his childhood in a Charleston orphanage. Benjamin, born of Jewish parents in the British West Indies, came to Louisiana and made a fortune practicing law. Mallory was born in Trinidad; his widowed mother had run a boardinghouse in Key West. Reagan had been an overseer. Alexander H. Stephens, the Vice President, was the son of a slaveless Georgia farmer. From Jefferson Davis on down, the so-called government of the cavaliers was run by men who were new to cavalier ways.

The government makers who met at Montgomery in February 1861 elected Davis and Stephens as provisional executives, and the delegates constituted themselves a provisional Congress. Later, in an election in which there was no opposition, the choices of Davis and Stephens were ratified as permanent. When Virginia seceded, the capital was moved to the more commodious spaces of Richmond. But before the men left Montgomery, they also drafted a permanent constitution for the new nation. This document reflected both the essential conservatism of the South and its devotion to states' rights.

THE structure of the Southern government was identical to that of the old Union. There was an executive branch headed by a President, a legislative branch made up of a two-house Congress and a judicial branch topped by a Supreme Court (although this court was never actually created). The framers of the government saw nothing odd in duplicating the machinery of the government they had departed from. In the Southern view, that machinery was satisfactory; it was the spirit of centralism that the North had introduced into the system that had corrupted it. In the new constitution, there were numerous provisions to ensure that the same result would not occur again.

The principle of state sovereignty was specifically recognized, although the right of secession was not specifically mentioned. The powers delegated to the general government were fewer and those reserved to the states greater than in the United States Constitution. Various clauses sanctified the South-

The slim 90-pound body of Confederate Vice President Alexander Stephens was barely strong enough to contain his raging hatreds. At various times he attacked the Union, the waltz, secession, Jefferson Davis and even "the whole human race." A Washington reporter called him "small and sick and sorrowful," and said that he would look the same dead as he did alive.

ern belief in the right of a minority to check the majority. A two-thirds vote of Congress was required to admit new states or enact important appropriation bills, and any three states could force a national convention to amend the constitution. Southerners thought that their constitution was a return to the original principles and purity of the old Constitution written at Philadelphia in 1787. Some of the delegates at the Montgomery convention seriously proposed to adopt the Stars and Stripes in modified form as the official banner, apparently on the ground that the South was the legal American government and the North the "rebellion." Indeed, the first Confederate flag bore a suspicious resemblance to the U.S. emblem, and a disgusted member of Congress wrote that it was difficult "to tear the people away entirely from the desire to appropriate some reminiscence of the old flag."

ONE of the great ironies of the Confederate adventure was that it was a conservative revolution that looked to the past rather than the future, that proposed to restore an ideal that had been rather than to create one that should be. The Confederacy set forth into the modern world with a government frankly based on 18th Century practices.

It was another irony that the Confederacy embarked on a modern war, with all the inner unity such a conflict demands, under a system that glorified localism and separatism. That principle of states' rights which the South held so sacred would in the end help to bring about the downfall of its attempt at nationhood. In the beginning, Southern opinion was strongly united; the great majority of the people were willing, although with varying degrees of intensity, to support the war until independence was won. The only organized resistance to the objectives of the war was in the mountain regions, notably in western Virginia—the part that in 1863 became the new state of West Virginia—and in eastern Tennessee. The mountain people were troublesome to the Confederacy and embarrassing to its boast of a unified South, but they were too small a minority to impede the conduct of the war.

But as the conflict continued—as Southern territory was occupied and defeats multiplied and victory receded—a profound war weariness settled over the masses. Toward the end a large segment of the population came to feel that the cause was hopeless and might as well be abandoned. Many people were bitterly convinced that their leaders were incompetent, that the government favored the rich over the poor—it was a war for slavery but the slaveholders were not pulling their weight—and that they were losing a war that could have been won. But even at the last all but the most disillusioned would have contended that the goal, Southern independence, was good.

There was unity as to the objectives of the war but discord as to how it should be waged. Some of the differences were the normal ones that would have appeared in any society engaged in a war. People—politicians, editors, ordinary citizens—criticized the government for military reverses, for picking the wrong generals, for supply shortages. The government resorted to some measures that caused certain classes to cry out that they were being discriminated against. Taxes in kind, or produce, were levied on farmers, and the government set its own prices on supplies it purchased, thereby evoking loud protests from the agricultural interests.

Trying to maintain home supervision of the slave labor force, the government permitted the exemption from military service of one white man on a

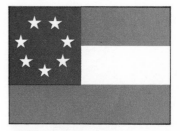

"STARS AND BARS"

BATTLE FLAG

"STAINLESS BANNER"

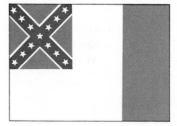

LAST OFFICIAL FLAG

The flags of the Confederacy are shown in order of adoption. The first, vaguely resembling the U.S. flag, was abandoned when Rebel troops fired on it by mistake. The second remained the soldiers' favorite, though the third became the national emblem in 1863. But from a distance this one looked objectionably like a flag of truce, so a red band was added (bottom).

A lady smuggler, one of many who packed their bustles and hoop-skirts with contraband for the South, is caught with some medicine by an inspector in Washington. Coffee and pistols were other choice prizes for the daring ladies, and at least one of them smuggled in rifles by the coffin load.

Spurning their civilian suitors, two ardent Rebel women push them to enlist. Such "fire-eaters" even put off soldier beaux until they proved their valor in battle. One girl reassured her man that if he got killed she would announce their engagement anyhow—"provided your wounds are all in the front."

plantation with 20 or more slaves. This law was a blatant example of class favoritism and aroused wide and angry condemnation from small slaveholders and farmers. "It's a rich man's war and a poor man's fight" became a bitter saying in the Confederacy. Despite the popular outcry against particular measures, the Davis Administration maintained a surprisingly tight control over the opposition in Congress. In contrast with Lincoln, who vetoed or pocket-vetoed only six bills, Davis vetoed 39 and made his decision stick in all but one. The Congress bowed to the presidential vetoes partly for reasons of patriotism—it seemed important not to show disunity—and partly because of apathy. But as critical newspapers implored Congress to stop acting as a "register of royal proclamations," the opposition mounted in strength; at the last, over 40 per cent of Congress was voting against Davis' measures.

CONFLICT over military issues stirred dissension without weakening the nation. Even the bitterness over who was bearing the burden did not greatly hamper the conduct of the war. But one issue rose that did hurt the war effort and was a major factor in causing the eventual collapse of the Confederacy. In another of those ironies that characterize the Southern venture, this was the question of states' rights, the great principle for which the South had left the Union. From their experience in the old Union many Southerners had become so accustomed to reacting against central controls that they could not bear to accept any, even those imposed by their own government.

States' rights and individualism were ideals to be cherished for their own sake rather than as means to an end. The strongest organized opposition to the Davis Administration came from advocates of states' rights who thought that the government was grasping at too much power. That the government was fighting a war and needed power impressed them not at all. They were patriotic Southerners and wanted the South to win its independence—but independence was not worth the surrender of state sovereignty. As between sacrifice of the great principle and defeat, they would take defeat.

Vice President Stephens, their titular leader, expressed perfectly their obsession with the abstract in an address to the Georgia legislature. "Never for a moment permit yourselves to look upon liberty . . . as subordinate to independence," he cried. "The one was resorted to to secure the other. . . . Let them stand together . . . and if such be our fate, let them and us all go down together in a common ruin. Without liberty, I would not turn upon my heel for independence." A strong Southern government, or as he put it, "a master from the South," was as bad as a strong Northern government. Southerners, he concluded, were not born to choose between masters.

The states' rights opposition was present in all states, but strongest in South Carolina, North Carolina and Georgia. In the last two states the governors acted boldly to obstruct the powers employed by the central government. The two chief exercises of power objected to by the states' righters were the suspension of habeas corpus in disaffected areas and the conscription of men into a national army. At first the objectors could only denounce the actions of the government as thinly veiled attempts to establish a dictatorship, and throw every possible impediment in the way of execution of the national laws. Sometimes these impediments were substantial. For example, governors could certify men in the state militia as exempt from conscription; in 1862 at least 100,000 men of draft age were held out in state service. It was estimated that in Georgia in 1864 more men between the ages of 18 and 45 were exempted than were drafted into the army.

As the war continued and the authority of the central government became weaker, the states' rights feeling became stronger. In the last stages some states defied the government to enforce its orders. Governor Joseph Brown of Georgia refused a request for the services of his militia. These troops, he coolly told Richmond, were the state's only defense against enemy invasion and Confederate domination. The insistence on states' rights did not in itself destroy the Confederacy, but it helped.

The states' rights philosophy, although clothed in legal language, was not merely an expression of legalism. It represented something deeper in Southern society. Southerners were intensely localistic and individualistic and in an extreme way democratic. Northerners, living in a more collective society, could accept the discipline required by modern war. For most Southerners this self-imposed discipline was difficult, and for some impossible. Even if the Confederacy had won its independence it could not have survived, unless it had been able to alter drastically the whole nature of Southern society.

When at the beginning of the war thoughtful Southerners contemplated the economic potential of the combatant powers, they were well aware of their side's inferiority in material resources. It was a deficiency that the Confederate government made frantic efforts to overcome. The war witnessed a substantial expansion of industrial facilities, and curiously, in view of the South's devotion to states' rights, most of the new facilities were the direct result of action by the central authority. The government established its own war plants; it subsidized private plants by lending them money to get started in return for a pledge to sell the bulk of their products to the government; and it stimulated the growth of existing plants, such as the large Tredegar Iron Works in Richmond, by the allocation of war contracts.

"The brains of the Confederacy," Judah P. Benjamin, "sphinx-like" and "enigmatic," served the Rebel cause as Attorney General, Secretary of War and Secretary of State. He had an odd mania for destroying his papers, and by dint of hard work at incineration he died leaving barely a scrap behind him.

THE principal figure in this government-sponsored program was Josiah Gorgas, director of ordnance and one of the great American production managers. Gorgas had a genius for organization and an uncanny ability to select the right subordinates. Under his supervision a complex of dispersed factories was set up, located mainly in Georgia, Alabama and the Carolinas. But even Gorgas' best efforts could not overcome the fatal Southern economic lag. There were distressing shortages of raw materials and skilled labor. By 1862 the largest Northern arsenals were capable of producing 5,000 rifles a day, while the Southern maximum, not often reached, was only 300 a day. The most serious handicap was the absence of machines and the consequent reliance on hand labor. The largest government depot turning out textiles employed 3,000 women to sew uniforms by hand. The largest shoe plant, utilizing the same kind of labor, could produce only 5,000 pairs a week in 1862 (though another was opened the following year with double that capacity). By contrast, Northern factories, using shoe-stitching machines patented in 1862, had manufactured 2.5 million pairs by the end of 1863.

Most plants in existence before the war were small, and even with the new facilities the Southern industrial system was unable to meet the needs of its armies and civilian population. Agricultural production fell off as large areas of territory were occupied and the slave labor force left the plantations with the approach of Federal armies. By 1863 serious shortages prevailed in both

Stephen Mallory, Confederate Secretary of the Navy, realized the South had plenty of captains but not enough warships, so he proposed building a fleet of ironclads in Europe. None of these ironclads was delivered, but the homemade "Merrimack" won the most notable of the South's victories at sea.

agriculture and industry, and after that date became progressively worse.

Even the army felt the pinch. A soldier at Port Hudson, Louisiana, recorded that for months the men had received no pork or flour and were on half-rations of rice and peas; one at Charleston, South Carolina, complained that the daily ration consisted of a small loaf of bread and a gill of sorghum. Even when supplies were available, they often could not be transported where they were needed because of the gradual collapse of the railroad system under the strain of war. Because of the concentration on weapons production, not a single new rail was rolled in the Confederacy. To supply the main lines, rails were uprooted from secondary roads, with the result that tracks into the food-raising areas almost disappeared. The reality of suffering and sacrifice and the sense of facing a foe with inexhaustible resources helped to lower mass morale in the final stages of the war.

With its simple economy, the South presented almost insuperable problems to those charged with financing its war. Like the Northern financial directors, Secretary Memminger and the congressional leaders approached the issue of war taxation timidly. Not until 1863 did Congress enact a general internal revenue measure, and because of low rates and poor enforcement it produced little income. Of its total revenue during the war, the government raised the appallingly small portion of 1 per cent from taxation.

The Treasury preferred the less painful method of borrowing and sold huge quantities of bonds. As an interesting experiment, some loans were subscribed in the form of produce—cotton, corn, livestock and the like. The produce loans were in part an attempt by the government to escape from its own paper currency. Again like the Northern government, the Confederacy, faced by the necessity to raise ready revenue, resorted to the issuance of paper money and treasury notes. But laboring under greater economic disabilities, the government continued to take the easy printing-press way and by the end of the war had put forth the tremendous total of two billion dollars or more in paper. States and cities and even business institutions also issued their own notes.

The result was a huge and confusing accumulation of money and an astronomical inflation of prices. One Richmond official estimated in 1863 that his salary of $3,000 bought no more than $300 would in ordinary times. A Confederate officer breakfasting in Richmond in 1864 was appalled to learn that the bill for three persons was $141. "How are our people to live?" he wondered.

German-born Christopher Gustavus Memminger brought little humor or imagination to a job which begged for much of both—Confederate Secretary of the Treasury. Funds were so low at first that he had to borrow a desk. During his term one billion dollars in paper money was printed. In the resultant inflation, the $500 bill at right brought as little as $10 in specie.

"The soldiers' wives and families?" Many people could have returned a grim answer. Another government employee wrote in his diary: "I cannot afford to have more than an ounce of meat daily for each member of my family of six. . . . The old cat goes staggering about from debility. . . . We see neither rats nor mice about the premises now. This is famine. Even the pigeons watch the crusts in the hands of the children, and follow them in the yard."

Still, despite its mistakes, some of which could not be avoided, the Confederacy performed a remarkable financial feat. The government, with never more than $27 million of specie, set a new nation in being, raised and equipped armies and navies, and held off a superior foe in four years of war. Even among long-established governments few have done so well with so little.

For those Europeans who might have been interested, the Confederate economic experience was a cruelly revealing illustration of the difficulties of an agricultural nation engaged in a modern war. Europeans were fascinated by the American conflict, but the economic example was lost on them. They saw the struggle not for what it was—a new kind of war, a war of supply and technology—but as a contest in the older tradition.

For their part, Southerners were deceived as to the interest of the powerful nations of Europe in the war. It was a staple item of Southern belief that the South would win its independence, even without the force of its own arms, because the European markets had to have cotton, and "King Cotton" would force Europe to intervene in the war on the Southern side. Southern diplomacy was at first confident and always aggressive and positive, devoted to securing recognition of the Confederacy as a nation and then to inducing England or France to force mediation on the North. Northern diplomacy was more negative. Its objectives were to forestall diplomatic recognition of what the North insisted was merely a rebellion and to prevent active European intervention in the war.

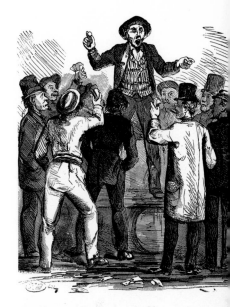

A gold piece, enormously valuable in the Confederacy, is sold to the highest bidder in a North Carolina auction. Practically all of the South's precious metal was drained off to buy arms abroad. Gold was so scarce, and Confederate paper money worth so little, that a line from Shakespeare became an oft-quoted wisecrack: "Who steals my purse steals trash."

THE key nations in the diplomatic picture were Great Britain and France. They were the two leading world powers, they were the only European nations whose interests could be directly affected by the outcome of the contest and they were the only countries which possessed the strength to intervene. Of the two, England was the more important. It and France operated together under an understanding that in specified areas the interests of one took precedence over the other. The United States was in the sphere of English influence, and therefore in the American war Britain would lead and France would follow. The French emperor, Napoleon III, was sympathetic to the Southern cause. "If the North is victorious, I shall be happy," he exclaimed; "if the South is victorious, I shall be enchanted." But in his actions he still conformed to the policy laid down in London. Even a rumor that the Confederacy would cede Texas to France in return for aid did not move him. The French foreign minister told the American minister: "France would not take Texas as a gift, even if it were accompanied by a handsome bribe besides."

Several factors would determine the course of the British government—not least that an auspicious opportunity for intervention never developed—but one of the most compelling was the opinion of its own people.

British opinion mirrored accurately the reactions of most of Europe to the American crisis. Upper-class and business opinion was on the whole sympathetic to the Confederacy. The landed gentry felt a social and cultural affinity to the plantation South. The manufacturing magnates thought that an independent Confederacy would open up a tariff-free Southern market to British exports. Moreover, both groups were fighting off demands by the masses for an extension of the suffrage, and if the South attained independence they could point to the divided republic as a proof that democracy would not work in a populous country. The existence of two American nations also would mean that neither would be able to dominate the Western Hemisphere. One or both would have to seek the support of Europe and would thus fall into the European power system.

But English and European opinion was puzzled by certain aspects of the American struggle, and the perplexity tended to dilute the first strong sympathy for the South. One of the great causes of 19th Century liberalism was nationalism, or self-determination, the right of a people to decide their own destiny under their own government. On the face of it the South seemed to be contending for exactly this principle. But then the South was also trying to destroy an established nation, and liberals wondered what the real issue was.

Confederate emissaries to Europe Slidell and Mason (center) are removed from a British ship by a U.S. officer. The seizure on the high seas embarrassed the Union, and there was talk of war with Britain. "Good God," the budding historian Henry Adams wrote from London, "what's got into you all?"

UNDERLYING all of European opinion was the question of slavery. Europe was intensely and almost universally antislavery, a fact which the South, insulated by its own choice from outside influences, was slow to appreciate. What most confused the liberals was that in the first half of the war the Northern government affected to be waging war not for the abolition of slavery but for political domination. But some men in England and in the countries of Europe saw from the first that the logic of events would turn the conflict into a crusade against slavery.

In Britain such middle-class leaders as John Bright supported the North primarily for this reason, and the laboring masses rallied behind them. In a famous pro-Northern speech, Bright declared: "Privilege thinks it has a great interest in this contest, and every morning, with blatant voice, it comes into your streets and curses the American Republic. Privilege has beheld an afflicting spectacle for many years past. It has beheld thirty millions of men, happy and prosperous, without emperor, without king . . . without great armies and great navies, without great debt and without great taxes. Privilege has shuddered at what might happen to old Europe if this grand experiment should succeed. But you, the workers . . . you struggling upwards towards the light . . . you have no cause to look with jealousy upon a country which, amongst all the great nations of the globe, is that one where labour has met with the highest honour, and where it has reaped its greatest reward." Once the North joined the causes of emancipation and nationalism, it would have a combination irresistible to Europeans.

In the end, inevitably, all the South's lustrous hopes crashed in frustration. England and France recognized the Confederacy as a belligerent but not as a nation, and the other European governments followed suit. No Confederate diplomat was ever received openly and officially as the representative of an accredited government, and midway in the war the Confederate minister to Britain deemed his treatment so humiliating that he left London for Paris. Nor could the Confederacy induce the great powers to intervene in the war.

There were episodes that might have brought intervention. In 1861 a Northern naval officer, Charles Wilkes, rashly stopped a British steamer, the *Trent*, and removed by force two Confederate diplomats, James Mason and John

Slidell, traveling to England and France. But the Lincoln government eventually assuaged Britain's outraged feelings by handing the diplomats back. The English government permitted the Confederacy to order from British shipyards vessels to prey on Northern ocean traffic. The Union government protested and after the war served England with a large damage claim which was paid after long negotiation. In 1863 the Confederacy also placed an order with English builders for two ironclad rams with which to break the blockade. If these ships had been delivered, war between Britain and the United States might well have followed. But the royal government, suddenly coming to its senses, halted delivery of the rams at the last moment.

Britain, it seems clear, failed to intervene in the American war for several reasons. The war did cut off the Southern cotton supply and hit the great English textile industry hard, but although the impact was injurious it was not fatal. Some cotton was imported from Egypt and India, and the textile workers who suffered the most from the depression were antislavery and still supported the North. The military situation never turned enough in favor of the South to render intervention safe. And finally, after Lincoln announced the Emancipation Proclamation neither England nor any other government would have dared to act for the South.

Perhaps the most sensational episode in Civil War diplomacy emanated from the restless, vaulting mind of the emperor of France, Napoleon III. Ambitious to restore the colonial glories of France and to cut an imperial figure on the world stage, he seized the opportunity provided by a divided America to set up a puppet empire in Mexico. His pretext was the failure of the Mexican government to repay a loan to French bankers. A French army landed and occupied the capital, Mexico City, as well as a substantial portion of the country. The United States, fearful of provoking France into recognizing the Confederacy, could only register a formal protest. But the Confederate government, hoping to secure French recognition, welcomed the intervention.

Many Southerners, however, condemned the French action and for a traditional American reason—it was a violation of the Monroe Doctrine. The remark of a Confederate soldier to a Union trooper in a moment of fraternizing between battles was typical: "We don't want any of their help—damn their frog-eating souls. If they interfere in our fight we-uns will turn in with you-uns and lick hell out of them." After the conflict the United States was able to pressure France out of Mexico. But if two American nations had emerged from the conflict neither would have been strong enough to have withstood European influence. The French adventure was an omen of what the future would have brought to a divided Union.

E UROPEAN liberals recognized the significance of the Civil War for the causes of nationalism and freedom. The Italian patriot Giuseppe Mazzini, rhetorically addressing the Union, exclaimed: "You have done more for us in four years than 50 years of teaching, preaching and writing from all your European brothers have been able to do." And a mass meeting in Brussels at the end of the war sent these greetings to a reunited America: "The whole world has been deeply moved by your successes. . . . These teachings which Young America gives us will not be lost on Old Europe. You have thus paved the way for universal brotherhood. You have strengthened the Union at home; we count upon you to cement the union of peoples."

John Slidell, Confederate envoy to France, reached there in 1862 none the worse for his rude detour (opposite). Formerly a New Yorker, Slidell was viewed by Unionists as a traitor. After the war, detested in the North and with no desire to share the tribulations of the defeated South, he remained abroad.

James Murray Mason, Confederate envoy to England, created a favorable impression among the British gentry though his enemies charged that he dressed shabbily and spat upon the floor of Parliament. In spite of his friends in high places, the British government never received him officially.

WATCHING WAR START, Rebel crowds gather on rooftops as guns fire from Fort Moultrie (*left*) and from Cummings Point (*right*) on Fort Sumter (*center*). There were mixed feelings; one witness heard "prayers from the women and imprecations from the men."

The Rebels' gallant, fruitless fight

THE South went gaily to war. On the eve of the bombardment of Fort Sumter, Mary Boykin Chesnut wrote from Charleston, she attended "the merriest, maddest dinner we have had yet," with all the men "audaciously wise and witty." The women yearned to help their men, if only by sewing, but in those first days the new soldiers of the South avoided amateur seamstresses whenever possible. Georgia's Hussars adorned their ranks in $25,000 worth of tailor-made gilt and glitter. The Granville Rifles paraded in firehouse-red shirts, the East Tennesseans in yellow jackets and the Orleans Guards in dress blues (they later wore the blue uniforms into battle at Shiloh and shortly found themselves fighting both sides).

But as time passed, these glories faded and natty "cadet" gray gave way to the dirty yellowish-brown called butternut. The Confederate army never lost a battle for want of shot and shell, but all else came in short supply, and Lee's troops fought hungry and marched in tatters. A Texan could boast that in his regiment one hole in the trousers indicated a captain, two holes a lieutenant and the seat all out meant a private. But they patched their pants with red swatches in the shapes of hearts, eagles and cannon, and marched on. Sometimes they went 60 miles on their bare feet—for they were also short of shoes.

DRESSING HER SOLDIER, a Confederate woman adjusts the havelock on his kepi. These sunguards, invented by General Sir Henry Havelock for British troops in India, were part of the regulation Southern uniform here illustrated, but few soldiers ever wore one. They preferred soft slouch hats, which, besides keeping off sun and rain, made good pillows at night.

Mustering men and supplies for a long, woeful war

CROSSING THE POTOMAC, Maryland residents slip South carrying supplies and weapons. This divided border state provided 20,000 soldiers for the Confederate army, 46,000 for the North.

FROM all corners of the old Union Southerners hurried home to stand by their states. The South's chief asset was an ardent people, profoundly sure that fierce fervor wins wars. They possessed skilled and daring military leadership, spirited soldiery, patriotic citizenry. They also boasted ingenious men who stayed for four long years in the North, smuggling southward the products from the enemy's booming factories.

All this stirred the heart of Adalbert John Volck, who had become famous as one of the first dentists in Baltimore to use porcelain in filling teeth. Now to his adopted Confederacy he lent a talented draftsman's pen and a loving eye—and soon he became much more famous for such pictures as those on these two pages, showing the South as it marshaled its strength for the battle.

CROSSING THE PLAINS, General Albert Sidney Johnston (in the foreground) and a party of homeward-bound Southern sympathizers get directions from an Indian. Commander of the Union's Department of the Pacific, he resigned when the South seceded. He led Southern armies in Tennessee and died at Shiloh—believing he had won a battle that in truth was lost.

144

COLLECTING METAL, Southerners contribute their church bells to the cause *(above)*. In some cases artillery batteries were named for churches that had provided the iron for their guns.

COLLECTING MEDICINE, Southerners unload drugs *(below)* smuggled through the Union lines. Drugs were swapped for cotton; bales worth $100 in the South sold in Boston for $950.

CONFEDERATE COTTON BURNERS on a Tennessee plantation are surprised by a Federal patrol. Anxious to convince Europeans they needed Southern cotton, Confederates tried to keep the fibers out of Northern hands, fearing the Northerners would export it. This sketch, intended for publication in a periodical, is marked with the artist's instructions to the engraver.

Lengthening shadows
behind the Southern lines

SLOWLY the war gripped the South. Mary Chesnut told her diary less and less about gay dinners in South Carolina; instead she wrote: "I know how it feels to die. . . . Someone calls out: 'Albert Sidney Johnston is killed.' My heart stands still." And she was not the only one grown empty. The foundations of Southern policy were crumbling away. It had seemed sure that England would never let the South go down. Almost five million Englishmen depended for their livelihoods on Southern cotton, and the power to give or withhold cotton was the South's trump card. It trumped nothing: England, where unemployment rose to two million at one time, wavered, then stood aside from the conflict.

At first guns for the troops, and civilian luxuries too, still came through the blockade. But as the North mustered more ships this flow stopped and prices climbed. A pair of boots cost $200, a pound of butter eight dollars. The blockade, sighed Mary Chesnut, was really "a stockade which hems us in with only the sky open to us."

BLOCKADED piers of Charleston are piled high with cotton and lined with imprisoned ships. Some vessels were still running the blockade, but the Union navy was tightening the net; the grim day when the port would be entirely closed was coming near.

FLOURISHING Tredegar, the Confederacy's biggest iron works, provides a rare scene of industrial might in the South. This Richmond factory made 1,100 cannon for the Confederacy plus other war material, despite stoppages caused by a fire and a strike.

147

When the armies invaded
the old mansion's halls

As the war years ground on, the Old South, of courtly elegance and hot tempers, of the soft and dreamy slave-tended life and the stern dueling code, suffered and all but died. Both the Old and the Young Master, often as not, were away with the army, and many of the great mansions of the aristocracy—like the two Virginia homes shown here—became military objectives, some to be damaged or burned out in battle.

But this was only part of a draining that would take nearly half of all the wealth in the South. As the blockade tightened and Federal forces occupied more of the productive areas, Southern suffering grew. Slaves ran off. Food became scarce. Staples disappeared. An ounce of meat a day, often mule meat, was considered ample. People ate rats. Jefferson Davis said he saw no reason not to, since he considered rats as good as squirrels.

A TIDEWATER MANOR, Westover *(above)*, ancestral home of the Byrd family on the James River near Richmond, serves as a Union signaling station during the 1862 Peninsular Campaign. Some of the outbuildings received battle wounds, and a sturdy platform for the signalmen was erected on the roof.

A POTOMAC SHOW PLACE, the Lee home, across the river from Washington, provides a background for posturing Federals. The house was guarded and word sent to Mrs. Lee that it was being tended. The Lees never returned to the house, now part of Arlington National Cemetery.

FREED SLAVES from Jefferson Davis' plantation near Vicksburg arrive at a Union camp. Thousands of ex-slaves poured into Federal posts, creating a problem for officials. Some of the fugitives were mustered in as soldiers, others employed as laborers.

149

"Just before the battle"

Southern soldiers while away the long hours in camp at Corinth, Mississippi, playing cards, cooking supper, writing home. Gambling and letter writing were popular diversions—though some soldiers hid their cards before going into battle, fearful that God might not be kind to a man killed with cards in his

pockets. Their letters, often only half literate, were filled with grumbling over rations: "Beef & bread," complained one man, "bread an beef upper crust under crust an crum Som Sugar & molasses when that is said all is said." Singing was also a favorite pastime. The most popular tune was "Home, Sweet Home."

Another, borrowed from the North, was poignantly prophetic: "Just Before the Battle, Mother." The Confederate soldiers who found camp life lazy and companionable during the first two years of the war would soon face a rude awakening. Ahead lay months of battles and bloodshed—and finally defeat.

CHRONOLOGY *A timetable of American and world events: 1849-1865*
(The narrative account of military events listed below appears in Volume 6)

WORLD EVENTS	EXPANSION and EXPLORATION	POLITICS	MILITARY	ECONOMICS and SCIENCE	THOUGHT and CULTURE
1849-90 William III reigns in Netherlands 1850 Dickens' *David Copperfield* published 1851 Discovery of gold at Ballarat starts Australian gold rush 1851 Spain suppresses revolt in Cuba 1852 Second French Republic ends with Louis Napoleon proclaiming Second French Empire 1853 Santa Anna restores dictatorship in Mexico 1853-56 Crimean War halts Russian attempt to secure a warm-water port 1854-63 Mohammed Said rules as *khedive* of Egypt	1849 California Gold Rush reaches peak 1849 Minnesota Territory organized 1850 California statehood 1850 New Mexico and Utah Territories formally organized 1851 San Francisco Vigilance Committee organized to secure order in the city 1853 Washington Territory organized 1853 Gadsden Purchase negotiated with Mexico 1854 Kansas and Nebraska Territories organized 1854 Congress passes Graduation Act, providing for accelerated sale of public lands	1849 Organization of the Order of the Star-Spangled Banner, precursor of the Know-Nothing party March 1849 Zachary Taylor inaugurated March 1849 Department of the Interior created Dec. 1849 Three-week battle over organization of the House reflects growing threat of disunion March 1850 John C. Calhoun dies April 1850 In Clayton-Bulwer Treaty, U.S. and Britain agree to joint control of any Central American canal July 1850 President Zachary Taylor dies; Millard Fillmore succeeds to presidency Sept. 1850 Compromise of 1850, embodying Fugitive Slave Act, passed by Congress Nov. 1852 Democrat Franklin Pierce elected President; last major appearance of Whig party 1854 Republican party organized March 1854 Commodore Perry negotiates treaty of amity and commerce with Japan May 1854 Kansas-Nebraska Act passed, providing for popular decision on slavery in Kansas Oct. 1854 Lincoln delivers "Peoria Speech," his first public denunciation of the institution of slavery Oct. 1854 Ostend Manifesto calls for U.S. seizure of Cuba if purchase attempts fail		1849-56 U.S. business expands greatly 1850 Census shows 23,261,000 inhabitants, a 35.9 per cent increase over 1840 1851 Irish immigration to U.S. reaches peak of 221,253 in one year 1851 Illinois Central becomes first land-grant railroad 1851 William Kelly develops a process for converting pig iron to steel 1852 American Pharmaceutical Association founded 1852 Elisha G. Otis invents first passenger elevator 1853 New York Central Railroad formed by consolidation of three New York lines 1853 Singer sewing-machine factory opens in New York City 1854 Brief financial panic interrupts general prosperity 1854 Immigration of 427,833 is largest annual total until 1873 1854 First commercial flour mill established in Minneapolis 1854-68 75,000 Chinese immigrant laborers enter U.S.	1849 Thoreau's essay on "Civil Disobedience" published 1850 Stephen Foster composes "De Camptown Races" 1850 Singer Jenny Lind makes her American debut under sponsorship of P T Barnum 1850 Nathaniel Hawthorne's *The Scarlet Letter* published 1851 Fugitive slaves Rachel Parker and Thomas Sims rescued by antislavery men in Baltimore and Boston 1851 Hungarian patriot Louis Kossuth tours U.S. 1851 Nathaniel Hawthorne's *House of the Seven Gables* published 1851 Herman Melville's *Moby Dick* published 1851 The yacht *America* beats British yachts to win the first contest for what is henceforth called The America's Cup 1851 Dancer Lola Montez begins American career 1852 Harriet Beecher Stowe's *Uncle Tom's Cabin* published 1852 Smithsonian Institution erected 1854 Timothy Shay Arthur's *Ten Nights in a Bar-Room* published

1855 Bloodshed in Kansas

WORLD EVENTS	EXPANSION and EXPLORATION	POLITICS	MILITARY	ECONOMICS and SCIENCE	THOUGHT and CULTURE
1855 Dr. Livingstone discovers Victoria Falls, Rhodesia 1855 Santa Anna finally overthrown by Mexican reformers 1855-81 Alexander II is czar of Russia 1857 Irish Republican Brotherhood (the Fenians) organized 1857-58 Great Indian Mutiny, or Sepoy Rebellion, results in end of Mogul Empire; British Crown rules India, dissolving East India Company 1857-58 British military action forces China to open ports for trading 1858 Benito Juárez heads Liberal government in Mexico	1856 First railroad bridge is built over the Mississippi River, at Davenport, Iowa 1858 Minnesota statehood 1858 First stagecoach line from St. Louis to the West Coast, making possible coast-to-coast travel by public conveyance	March 1855 Kansas territorial elections, marked by fraud and violence, produce proslavery legislature Nov. 1855 Free-Soil convention in Kansas drafts antislavery constitution Jan. 1856 Kansas free-staters elect antislavery governor and legislature, creating dual government in territory May 1856 Senator Charles Sumner delivers "Crime against Kansas" speech, is beaten up by Representative Preston Brooks May 1856 Town of Lawrence, Kansas, attacked by proslavery raiders May 1856 John Brown's Pottawatomie, Kansas, massacre Nov. 1856 James Buchanan elected President over John C. Frémont, first candidate of the Republican party March 1857 Supreme Court hands down Dred Scott decision Oct. 1857 Free State party wins majority of legislature in Kansas territorial elections Aug.-Oct. 1858 Lincoln-Douglas debates highlight Illinois senatorial race Nov. 1858 Republicans win congressional elections in all Northern states but Illinois and Indiana		1855 Opening of the Soo Canal between Lakes Superior and Huron provides cheap transportation for iron ore 1856 Gail Borden patents process for condensed milk 1858 Lyman Blake patents machine to sew shoe soles to uppers 1858 Cyrus Field completes first transatlantic cable, which breaks down after three weeks 1859 American industrial production equals agricultural production for first time	1855 Verdi's *Il Trovatore* receives first U.S. performance 1855 Henry W. Longfellow's *Song of Hiawatha* published 1855 First kindergarten in U.S. opens at Watertown, Wisconsin 1855 Walt Whitman's *Leaves of Grass* published 1856 John Lothrop Motley's *Rise of the Dutch Republic* published 1857 J. S. Pierpont composes "Jingle Bells" 1857 Lithographers Nathaniel Currier and James Ives enter partnership as print publishers 1857 *Atlantic Monthly* and *Harper's Weekly* begin publication 1858 Oliver Wendell Holmes Sr.'s *Autocrat of the Breakfast Table* published 1858 National Association of Baseball Players, first governing body for the sport, formed 1859 Operatic debut of Adelina Patti, Italian-American soprano

1859 ... Cathedral begun in New York

1859 Daniel D. Emmett composes the song "Dixie"

1859 First American performances of Richard Wagner's *Tannhäuser* and *Lohengrin*

1860 Stephen Foster's "Old Black Joe" published

1860 First American performance of Verdi's *Rigoletto*

1861 First newspaper syndicate organized

1861 Winslow Homer joins McClellan's army as special artist for *Harper's Weekly*

1862 Publication of Julia Ward Howe's "Battle Hymn of the Republic"

1862 Morrill Land Grant Act provides federal aid to states to endow agricultural and technical colleges

1863 Publication of Civil War song "When Johnny Comes Marching Home"

1865 Mark Twain's short story "The Celebrated Jumping Frog of Calaveras County" published

1865 Mary Mapes Dodge's *Hans Brinker; or the Silver Skates* published

---

... well at Titusville, Pennsylvania, marks birth of modern oil industry

1860 Census shows 31,443,000 inhabitants, a 35.6 per cent increase over 1850

1860 Shoemakers' strike involves 20,000 workers in New England

1860 Oliver Winchester introduces the repeating rifle

1861 Morrill Tariff raises duties generally, with low-tariff Southerners no longer in Congress

1861 Confederacy issues first bank notes

1861 Dorothea Dix appointed superintendent of women nurses for Union army

1862 First federal income tax

1862 First issue of greenbacks

1862 Department of Agriculture established

1862 Richard J. Gatling perfects the revolving machine gun

1862 Jay Cooke floats large Civil War loan using patriotic appeals and advertising techniques

1863 Confederate Congress enacts general internal revenue act

1864 Northern Pacific Railroad chartered

1864 Railway mail service begins

1865 Congress imposes a tax on state bank notes; 700 state banks forced to become national banks, thus bringing about a uniform currency

---

March 1859 Supreme Court upholds Fugitive Slave Act

Oct. 1859 John Brown's raid on Harpers Ferry

1860 Southern legislatures proclaim right of secession

Nov. 1860 Abraham Lincoln elected President in four-way race

Dec. 1860 South Carolina secedes from Union

Dec. 1860 Crittenden resolutions die in committee

April 1861 Confederates fire on Fort Sumter

April 1861 Lincoln orders naval blockade of Confederacy

July 1861 First battle of Bull Run

Nov. 1861 Confederate commissioners removed from British ship *Trent*

April 1862 Confederate Conscription Act

April 1862 Battle of Shiloh

April-July 1862 Peninsular Campaign

Sept. 1862 Lee's first invasion of the North; battle of Antietam

March 1863 Union Conscription Act

March-July 1863 Vicksburg campaign

June-July 1863 Lee's second invasion of the North; battle of Gettysburg

July 1863 New York City draft riots

Sept. 1863 British bar delivery of British-built warships to Rebels; French follow suit

Oct.-Nov. 1863 Chattanooga campaign

March 1864 Grant takes supreme command of Union armies

May-June 1864 Wilderness Campaign

May-Sept. 1864 Atlanta campaign

June 1864-April 1865 Siege of Petersburg

Nov.-Dec. 1864 Sherman's march to the sea

April 1865 Lee surrenders

Jan.-Feb. 1861 Mississippi, Florida, Alabama, Georgia, Louisiana, Texas secede from Union

Feb. 1861 Delegates of seven seceding states, meeting at Montgomery, Alabama, draft Confederate Constitution, elect Jefferson Davis provisional President

Feb. 1861 Virginia peace convention attempts to heal the breach

April-May 1861 Virginia, Arkansas, Tennessee, North Carolina secede; Confederacy, now complete, numbers 9,103,000 people, Union 22,340,000

June 1862 U.S. recognizes Republic of Liberia

Sept. 1862 Lincoln issues Emancipation Proclamation to take effect Jan. 1, 1863

March 1863 Congress authorizes Lincoln to suspend right of habeas corpus

April 1863 Slavery abolished in the District of Columbia

June 1864 Fugitive Slave Act repealed

July 1864 Lincoln pocket-vetoes Wade-Davis bill for Radical Reconstruction

Nov. 1864 Lincoln re-elected President

Dec. 1864 Salmon P. Chase named Chief Justice of the U.S.

Feb. 1865 13th Amendment abolishing slavery submitted to states for ratification

April 1865 Lincoln assassinated by John Wilkes Booth; Andrew Johnson takes oath as President

---

1859 Oregon statehood

1859 Pikes Peak gold rush in Colorado

1859 Gold discovered in Comstock Lode, Nevada

1860 Pony Express starts mail runs from St. Joseph, Missouri, to Sacramento, California

1861 Kansas statehood

1861 Colorado, Nevada and Dakota Territories organized

1861 Telegraph lines link East and West coasts

1862 Homestead Act

1862 Great Sioux Uprising in Minnesota

1863 West Virginia statehood

1863 Idaho and Arizona Territories organized

1863 Montana gold rush

1864 Militia massacres Indians at Sand Creek, Colorado

1864 Nevada statehood

1864 Montana Territory organized

1859 Revolution in Haiti

1859 Ferdinand de Lesseps begins work on Suez Canal

1859 France and the Italian kingdom of Piedmont go to war against Austria

1859 Charles Darwin's *Origin of Species* published

1861 The Civil War

1861 Czar Alexander's Emancipation Edict frees Russian serfs

1861 Kingdom of Italy is formed with Victor Emmanuel as king

1861 Prince Albert of Britain dies

1861-76 Abdul Aziz reigns in Ottoman Empire

1861-88 William I reigns in Prussia

1861-89 Louis I rules Portugal

1862-90 Otto Von Bismarck serves as Minister-President of Prussia, later Chancellor of German Empire

1863 International Committee of the Red Cross is organized

1863 French troops occupy Mexico City

1863 French establish protectorate over Cambodia

1863-64 Polish revolution against Russia suppressed

1863-1906 Christian IX reigns in Denmark

1863-1913 George I reigns in Greece

1864 Maximilian is crowned emperor of Mexico

1864 Prussia, Austria war with Denmark over Schleswig and Holstein

1865 Lewis Carroll's *Alice's Adventures in Wonderland* published

1865-1909 Leopold II reigns in Belgium

FOR FURTHER READING

These books were selected for their interest and authority in the preparation of this volume, and for their usefulness to readers seeking additional information on specific points. An asterisk (*) marks works available in both hard-cover and paperback editions; a dagger (†) indicates availability only in paperback. Books dealing with battles and strategy are listed in Volume 6.

GENERAL READING

Angle, Paul (ed.), *The Lincoln Reader*. Rutgers University Press, 1947.

Butterfield, Roger, *The American Past*. Simon and Schuster, 1957.

Carman, Harry J., Harold C. Syrett and Bernard W. Wishy, *A History of the American People*, Vol. I. Alfred A. Knopf, 1960.

Cole, Arthur C., *The Irrepressible Conflict, 1850-1865*, Vol. VI, *History of American Life*. Macmillan, 1934.

Craven, Avery O., *The Coming of the Civil War*. University of Chicago Press, 1957.

Davidson, Marshall, *Life in America* (2 vols.). Houghton Mifflin, 1951.

Eaton, Clement, *A History of the Old South*. Macmillan, 1949.

Hicks, John Donald, *The Federal Union; A History of the United States to 1877*. Houghton Mifflin, 1957.

Malone, Dumas, and Basil Rauch, *Empire for Liberty*, Vol. I. Appleton-Century-Crofts, 1960.

Morison, Samuel Eliot, and Henry Steele Commager, *The Growth of the American Republic*, Vol. I. Oxford University Press, 1962.

†Nichols, Roy Franklin, *The Disruption of American Democracy*. Collier, 1962.

Pratt, Julius W., *A History of United States Foreign Policy*. Prentice-Hall, 1955.

Randall, James G., and David Donald, *The Civil War and Reconstruction*. D. C. Heath, 1961.

Wilson, Mitchell A., *American Science and Invention, a Pictorial History*. Bonanza Books, 1960.

CRISIS AND SECESSION (CHAPTERS 1, 2, 3, 4, 5)

Ashley, Clifford W., *The Yankee Whaler*. Halcyon House, 1942.

Beveridge, Albert J., *Abraham Lincoln, 1809-1858* (2 vols.). Houghton Mifflin, 1928.

*Buckmaster, Henrietta, *Let My People Go*. Peter Smith, 1959.

Capers, Gerald M., *Stephen A. Douglas, Defender of the Union*. Little, Brown, 1959.

Channing, Edward, *A History of the United States*, Vol. VI, *The War for Southern Independence*. Macmillan, 1927.

*Coit, Margaret L., *John C. Calhoun, American Portrait*. Houghton Mifflin, 1950.

*Current, Richard N., *Daniel Webster and the Rise of National Conservatism*. Little, Brown, 1955.

Dodd, William E., *The Cotton Kingdom*. Yale University Press, 1919.

Donald, David, *Charles Sumner and the Coming of the Civil War*. Alfred A. Knopf, 1960.

Dulles, Foster Rhea, *America Learns to Play: A History of Popular Recreation, 1607-1940*. Peter Smith, 1952. *Lowered Boats*. Harcourt, Brace & World, 1933.

Fuess, Claude M., *Daniel Webster* (2 vols.). Little, Brown, 1930.

Gray, L.C., *History of Agriculture in the Southern United States to 1860*. Peter Smith, 1942.

Hamilton, Holman, *Zachary Taylor* (2 vols.). Bobbs-Merrill, 1941-1951.

Klein, Philip Shriver, *President James Buchanan*. Pennsylvania State University Press, 1962.

Korngold, Ralph, *Two Friends of Man*. Little, Brown, 1950.

McDermott, John Francis, *George Caleb Bingham, River Portraitist*. University of Oklahoma Press, 1959.

Monaghan, Jay, *Civil War on the Western Border, 1854-1865*. Little, Brown, 1955.

Nevins, Allan, *The Ordeal of the Union* (2 vols.). Charles Scribner's Sons, 1947.

Nichols, Roy Franklin, *Franklin Pierce, Young Hickory of the Granite Hills*. University of Pennsylvania Press, 1958.

*Parrington, Vernon Louis, *Main Currents in American Thought* (3 vols.). Harcourt, Brace & World, 1939.

*Phillips, Ulrich B., *Life and Labor in the Old South*. Little, Brown, 1929.

*Potter, David M., *Lincoln and His Party in the Secession Crisis*. Yale University Press, 1942.

*Sandburg, Carl, *Abraham Lincoln: The Prairie Years* (2 vols.). Harcourt, Brace & World, 1928.

Stackpole, Edouard A., *Sea-Hunters*. J. B. Lippincott, 1953.

Stampp, Kenneth M., *And the War Came*. Louisiana State University Press, 1950.

Sydnor, Charles S., *The Development of Southern Sectionalism, 1819-1848*, Vol. V, *History of the South*. Louisiana State University Press, 1948.

Taylor, George R., *The Transportation Revolution: 1815-1860*. Holt, Rinehart & Winston, 1951.

Thomas, Benjamin P., *Abraham Lincoln, a Biography*. Alfred A. Knopf, 1952.

Wiltse, Charles M., *John C. Calhoun* (3 vols.). Bobbs-Merrill, 1944-1951.

THE WARRING REGIONS (CHAPTERS 6, 7)

Adams, Ephraim D., *Great Britain and the American Civil War*. Peter Smith, 1957.

American Heritage Picture History of the Civil War. The American Heritage, 1960.

*Current, Richard N., *The Lincoln Nobody Knows*. McGraw-Hill, 1958.

*Donald, David, *Lincoln Reconsidered*. Alfred A. Knopf, 1956.

Duberman, Martin B., *Charles Francis Adams, 1807-1886*. Houghton Mifflin, 1961.

*Hendrick, Burton J., *Lincoln's War Cabinet*. Peter Smith, 1961. *Statesmen of the Lost Cause; Jefferson Davis and His Cabinet*. Little, Brown, 1939.

*Jones, John B., *A Rebel War Clerk's Diary*, ed. by Earl Schenck Miers. Sagamore Press, 1958.

Klement, Frank L., *Copperheads in the Middle West*. University of Chicago Press, 1960.

Nevins, Allan, *The Emergence of Lincoln* (2 vols.). Charles Scribner's Sons, 1950. *The War for the Union* (2 vols.). Charles Scribner's Sons, 1959-1960.

Owsley, Frank L. and Harriet C., *King Cotton Diplomacy*. University of Chicago Press, 1959.

Randall, James G., *Lincoln the President*, Vol. IV with Richard N. Current. Dodd, Mead, 1945-1955.

*Sandburg, Carl, *Abraham Lincoln: The War Years* (4 vols.). Harcourt, Brace, 1939.

*Sideman, Belle B., and Lillian Friedman (eds.), *Europe Looks at the Civil War*. Orion Press, 1960.

Simkins, Francis B., and James Welch Patton, *The Women of the Confederacy*. Garret and Massie, 1936.

Strode, Hudson, *Jefferson Davis* (2 vols.). Harcourt, Brace & World, 1955-1959.

Todd, Richard Cecil, *Confederate Finance*. University of Georgia Press, 1954.

Wilson, Edmund, *Patriotic Gore: Studies in the Literature of the American Civil War*. Oxford University Press, 1962.

Yearns, Wilfred Buck, *The Confederate Congress*. University of Georgia Press, 1960.

ACKNOWLEDGMENTS

The author wishes to thank Frank E. Vandiver, Professor of History, Rice University, for his assistance. The editors of this book are particularly indebted to James P. Shenton, Associate Professor of History, Columbia University, for his valuable assistance and advice. They are also grateful to Albert K. Baragwanath, Curator of Prints, Museum of the City of New York; Paul Bride, The New-York Historical Society; Eleanor S. Brockenbrough and India W. Thomas, Confederate Museum, Richmond, Virginia; Edward M. Davis III, The Valentine Museum, Richmond, Virginia; Margaret A. Flint, Illinois State Historical Library, Springfield, Illinois; Roberts Jackson, The Bettmann Archive, New York City; Milton Kaplan and Carl Stange, Library of Congress, Washington, D.C.; R. Gerald McMurtry, Director, The Lincoln National Life Foundation, Fort Wayne, Indiana; Sol Novin, Culver Pictures, Inc., New York City; Philip F. Purrington, Curator, Old Dartmouth Historical Society and Whaling Museum, New Bedford, Massachusetts; Edouard A. Stackpole, Marine Historical Association, Mystic, Connecticut; Ross E. Taggart, Senior Curator, William Rockhill Nelson Gallery of Art, Atkins Museum of Fine Arts, Kansas City, Missouri; Wayne C. Temple, Director, Department of Lincolniana, Lincoln Memorial University, Harrogate, Tennessee; Hermann Warner Williams Jr., Director, Corcoran Gallery of Art, Washington, D.C.; John Francis McDermott; and Judy Higgins.

PICTURE CREDITS

The sources for the illustrations in this book are shown below. Credits for pictures from left to right are separated by semicolons, top to bottom by dashes. Sources have been abbreviated as follows: Bettmann—The Bettmann Archive; Brown—Brown Brothers; Culver—Culver Pictures; LC—Library of Congress; N-YHS—The New-York Historical Society, N.Y.C.; NYPL—The New York Public Library; N.Y. State Hist. Assn.—New York State Historical Association, Cooperstown.

CHAPTER 1: 6—Courtesy of The White House. 8, 9—Courtesy Museum of The City of New York; courtesy American Antiquarian Society, Worcester, Mass. 10, 11—Culver; Culver—Bettmann; Goodyear Tire and Rubber Company. 12, 13—Culver; Bettmann. 14, 15—Bettmann. 16, 17—Sy Seidman; Bettmann—Bettmann; Culver. 18, 19—Native Sons of Kansas City, courtesy William Rockhill Nelson Gallery of Art; collection City Art Museum of St. Louis. 20, 21—Collection City Art Museum of St. Louis except bottom right collection of Senator Claiborne Pell. 22, 23—The Metropolitan Museum of Art, Morris K. Jesup Fund, 1933. 24, 25—The Brooklyn Museum; Nelson Gallery—Atkins Museum, Nelson Funds, Kansas City, Mo.—Peabody Museum, Harvard University; private collection. 26, 27—Courtesy St. Louis Mercantile Library, copyright 1959 by the University of Oklahoma Press. 28, 29—Jahn & Ollier Engraving Co., collection of The Boatmen's National Bank of St. Louis.

CHAPTER 2: 30—Courtesy of The White House. 32, 33, 34—Bettmann. 35—Culver. 36, 37—NYPL; Bettmann. 39—Bettmann. 40, 41—The Whaling Museum, New Bedford, Mass.; The Whaling Museum, New Bedford, Mass., courtesy American Heritage Publishing Co., Inc. 42, 43—The Whaling Museum, New Bedford, Mass. except top left Herbert Orth, mural at Mystic Seaport, Marine Historical Association. 44 through 47—The Whaling Museum, New Bedford, Mass.

CHAPTER 3: 48—Courtesy of The White House and American Heritage Publishing Co., Inc. 50, 51—Bettmann except top right Culver. 52, 53—Culver. 54, 55—Bettmann except right Culver. 56—Culver except center Bettmann. 57—Bettmann. 58, 59—Courtesy Harry Shaw Newman, The Old Print Shop, Inc., N.Y.C.; Harvard Theatre Collection, courtesy American Heritage Publishing Co., Inc. 60, 61—National Baseball Hall of Fame, Cooperstown, N.Y.—*Bare Knuckles* by George A. Hayes, National Gallery of Art, Washington, D.C., collection of Edgar William and Bernice Chrysler Garbisch; Bradley Smith—Culver, 62—Culver—courtesy Museum of The City of New York. 63—Harvard Theatre Collection. 64, 65—Fernand Bourges, Museum of Fine Arts, Boston, M. & M. Karolik Collection.

CHAPTER 4: 66—Courtesy of The White House. 68, 69—Culver except top right Bettmann. 70, 71—Culver. 72, 73—Bettmann except left N.Y. State Hist. Assn. 74—Top: E. I. Du Pont De Nemours & Company, 75—Bettmann. 76, 77—Bettmann; from Stefan Lorant's *Lincoln, A Picture Story of His Life* (Harper). 78, 79—Culver. 80, 81—Culver; Don Richards. 82, 83—The Brooklyn Museum; The Cincinnati Art Museum. 84—Culver—N-YHS. 85—N-YHS; Sy Seidman—courtesy LC. 86—No credit—Brown. 87—Herbert Orth, The Metropolitan Museum of Art, Gift of Mr. and Mrs. Carl Stoeckel, 1897.

CHAPTER 5: 88—*President James Buchanan* by George P.A. Healy, National Gallery of Art, Washington, D.C., Mellon Collection. 90, 91—Bettmann; N-YHS. 92 through 95—Bettmann. 96—Collection George Eastman House, Rochester, N.Y., Gift of Alden Scott Boyer—Bettmann. 97—Henry E. Huntington Library, San Marino, Calif. 98, 99—Bettmann. 100, 101—Culver; Brown. 102—Left: The Lincoln National Life Foundation, Fort Wayne, Ind.—Kennedy Galleries, New York; right: Gjon Mili, original painting, Chicago Historical Society. 103—The Meserve Collection—Bettmann. 104, 105—Courtesy LC; The Meserve Collection—George Eastman House; courtesy of the Maryland Historical Society. 106, 107—Left: courtesy Harry Shaw Newman, The Old Print Shop, Inc., N.Y.C.; center: Culver—Bettmann; right: from Stefan Lorant's *Lincoln, A Picture Story of His Life* (Harper)—Culver. 108, 109—Courtesy Harry Shaw Newman, The Old Print Shop, Inc., N.Y.C.; The Meserve Collection.

CHAPTER 6: 110—Courtesy collection of Mrs. McCook Knox, Washington, D.C., and American Heritage Publishing Co., Inc. 112, 113—Bettmann. 114—From the collection of Norm Flayderman, Greenwich, Conn. 115—NYPL—Culver. 116, 117—Bettmann except top left Culver. 118, 119—Bettmann except right Culver. 120,121—Sy Seidman except right Culver. 122, 123—Sy Seidman; Herbert Orth, Berry-Hill Galleries. 124, 125—Herbert Orth, N-YHS; Sy Seidman. 126, 127—Herbert Orth, N-YHS; Herbert Orth, courtesy Lester S. Levy Collection—Herbert Orth, courtesy N.S. Meyer, Inc. 128, 129—Robert Huntzinger; collection of Alexander McCook Craighead, Dayton, Ohio, courtesy American Heritage Publishing Co., Inc.

CHAPTER 7: 130—Courtesy of Confederate Museum, Richmond, Va. 132—Bettmann. 133—Culver—Valentine Museum, Richmond, Va. 134, 135—Culver; drawings by Lewis Zacks. 136, 137—Culver—Bettmann; NYPL. 138—NYPL—Robert W. Kelley. 139—Culver. 140, 141—Culver except left Bettmann. 142, 143—LC; courtesy of Confederate Museum, Richmond, Va. 144—Courtesy of the Maryland Historical Society. 145—Courtesy LC. 146, 147—Houghton Library, Harvard University; courtesy of The South Carolina Historical Society, Charleston, S.C.—courtesy LC. 148, 149—Left: The National Archives; right: in the collection of The Corcoran Gallery of Art—N-YHS. 150, 151—Chapman Collection, Valentine Museum, Richmond, Va., courtesy American Heritage Publishing Co., Inc.

INDEX

*This symbol in front of a page number indicates a photograph or painting of the subject mentioned.
Military events are indexed in detail in Volume 6.